HOBBITS,
ELVES, AND
WIZARDS

HOBBITS, ELVES, AND WIZARDS

Exploring the Wonders
and Worlds of
J. R. R. Tolkien's
The Lord of the Rings

MICHAEL N. STANTON

palgrave
macmillan

HOBBITS, ELVES, AND WIZARDS
Copyright © Michael N. Stanton, 2001.
All rights reserved. No part of this book may be used or reproduced in any manner whatsoever without written permission except in the case of brief quotations embodied in critical articles or reviews.

First published in hardcover in 2001 by palgrave
First PALGRAVE MACMILLAN™ paperback edition: September 2002
175 Fifth Avenue, New York, N.Y. 10010 and
Houndmills, Basingstoke, Hampshire, England RG21 6XS.
Companies and representatives throughout the world.

PALGRAVE MACMILLAN is the global academic imprint of the Palgrave Macmillan division of St. Martin's Press, LLC and of Palgrave Macmillan Ltd. Macmillan® is a registered trademark in the United States, United Kingdom and other countries. Palgrave is a registered trademark in the European Union and other countries.

ISBN 1–4039–6025–9

Library of Congress Cataloguing-in-Publication Data available at the Library of Congress

A catalogue record for this book is available from the British Library.

Design by Letra Libre, Inc.

First PALGRAVE MACMILLAN paperback edition: September 2002
10 9 8 7 6 5 4 3 2 1

Printed in the United States of America.

In Memory of My Parents

Thomas
(1886–1955)
and
Genevieve
(1915–2000)

And of My Student and
Fellow Lover of Tolkien

Christopher J. Hill
(1961–1990)

TABLE OF CONTENTS

ACKNOWLEDGEMENTS

I wrote the first form of this book during a medical leave from teaching at the University of Vermont in the spring of 1997. I wrote it to entertain and instruct myself and sought neither encouragement nor warning; thus, the core of the book has been my responsibility from the start. Since that early draft, however, I have had help in altering the book considerably and, I hope, improving it somewhat.

For their help in the process, including suggestions, corrections, and words of encouragement, I thank my colleagues at UVM and elsewhere, including Virginia Clark, David Critchett, Chris Hansen, Mary Lou Kete, Alfred Rosa, Robyn Warhol, and Jamie Williamson. Special thanks go to Spencer Mallozzi, who read an early draft and gave me an honest reaction to it from a student's point of view; Spencer also helped me prepare a book proposal when the time came.

Once the book left my desk, my agent Michael Rosenberg of the Rosenberg Group helped me greatly and represented me ably. My editor Michael Flamini gave me wise counsel and encouragement in the right proportions. Mark Fowler helped make the book a reality as it now exists, and so in another sense did my nephew Alex Weinhagen, who solved a variety of computer mysteries for me. Other helpful suggestions came from Lydia Johnson, Mary Keesling, and Mark O'Brien.

In the background are scholars and writers whose work has been useful to me in diverse ways, and acknowledgement of whom in the notes and in the Bibliography can scarcely repay my debt. They include the earlier critics of Tolkien, such as Paul Kocher and Randel Helms, whose ideas are basic and even now important. Humphrey Carpenter's edition of the *Letters,* like his biography of Tolkien, has been a valuable resource. Everyone concerned with Tolkien owes a great debt to Christopher Tolkien and his compilation of *The History of Middle-earth;* it is work which for once deserves the term "monumental."

Above all I must thank the many many students who learned about Tolkien with me, and taught me about Tolkien, over the years in the classroom. The book is theirs in important ways, but needless to say, opinions expressed and errors committed in the book are entirely my own, as all concerned will readily concede.

PREFACE

This book is an attempt to put together in one place as much as I can of what I have learned in over twenty-five years of teaching J. R. R. Tolkien's *The Lord of the Rings*. The book does not attempt to expound any grand theory or set of critical principles; it tries only to make clear what readers of Tolkien's tale would want made clear for their greater enjoyment.

Little here is new. Even a modest structure like this book must build on the work of writers, readers, and scholars from years gone by, and my debt to others is acknowledged as fully as research and memory will allow. My greatest debt, however, is to the many hundreds of students who have taught me so much over the years.

Readers approach *The Lord of the Rings* from many directions. Some value it as a treasure house of imaginative linguistics; others see it in terms of myth; some as a muted religious statement; or as a latter-day version of heroic myth. All of these possibilities will get their due here, but for myself, I have always respected it most as a work of literary art, a fiction crafted by a master artist, and I have talked about it in terms of structure, unity, character depiction, theme, setting, fable, and the like. I respect *The Lord of the Rings* for its art, much as Tolkien taught us all to respect *Beowulf.*

My own relationship with *The Lord of the Rings* dates from its first paperback appearance in the United States, in 1965. I first read the pirated Ace paperbacks and then (trying to respect Tolkien's wishes) the authorized Ballantine paperback edition. The story drew me in, and I spent many hours in Middle-earth. I have been back many times since. One reason this book seemed worth doing is that I have always had to keep in mind that students were approaching Tolkien for the first or second time, not the twenty-first or -second, and that their questions needed considered answers.

Those questions have been about *The Lord of the Rings* itself. In answering them in the classroom, or here, I have tried to focus on that fiction and its appendices, and to bring in earlier work (work developed earlier in Tolkien's imagination but published later, like *The Silmarillion*) only as strictly necessary. It is easy—and pleasant—to get side-tracked. As Tolkien himself said in his "Foreword," *The Lord of the Rings* is the story of the War of the Rings, yet it includes "many glimpses" of the times that came before. (I, viii; *8*)* To try to clarify those glimpses only in relation to this text was the task I set myself, as a student among students.

I hope readers will find this book useful, and I hope that some of its utility will derive from its being enjoyable. It always was and still is a pleasure for me to talk about and write about *The Lord of the Rings,* and I hope that pleasure shows through.

---

*Parenthetical references to the text of *The Lord of the Rings* refer first to Part I, Part II, or Part III, then to the page number in the Ballantine paperback first issued in 1965, then, in *italics,* to the Del Rey/Ballantine paperback currently available.

PART I

One

BACKGROUNDS

BIOGRAPHICAL SKETCH
AND LITERARY CONTEXT

These are some of the externals of Tolkien's life; we can go back and see how various elements in this sketch fit into the creation of his book.

John Ronald Reuel Tolkien was born on January 3, 1892, the elder son of Arthur and Mabel (Suffield) Tolkien, in Bloemfontein, South Africa, where his father worked for the Bank of Africa. After a long and productive career spent largely in literary study, teaching, and writing, J. R. R. Tolkien died September 2, 1973, in the English resort town of Bournemouth.[1]

After the birth of Tolkien's brother Hilary in 1894, Mabel Tolkien returned with the boys to England, where in February 1896 word came that their father had died. Tolkien was brought up in large part in a quiet English village called Sarehole. Sarehole was a friendly, old-fashioned sort of village; its pleasant pastoral quality and rustic inhabitants helped shape Tolkien's vision of the Shire and its inhabitants.

His childhood contained another tragic event—his mother died before he was twelve; but he cherished her memory and never forgot that she had introduced him to his Roman Catholic religious faith and to the study of languages, both of which, in very different ways, sustained him all his life. After Mabel Tolkien's death, Ronald and Hilary came under the guardianship of Father Francis Morgan and were raised in the home of an aunt.

Tolkien graduated from Exeter College, Oxford, in 1915 and almost immediately went into military service in World War I as a second lieutenant in the Lancashire Fusiliers. When he was on sick leave, recuperating from trench fever in early 1917, he committed to paper the first elements of a story cycle, parts of which later became *The Silmarillion,* the first bud on the great tree of Middle-earth.

From 1918 to 1920 he was one of several assistant editors on the *OED,* as the *Oxford English Dictionary* is familiarly called. From 1920 to 1925 he was first Reader (assistant professor) and then Professor of English at the University of Leeds.

From 1925 to 1945 he was a fellow of Pembroke College, Oxford, with the title of Rawlinson and Bosworth Professor of Anglo-Saxon. In 1945 he changed colleges, becoming a fellow of Merton College, and Merton Professor of English Language and Literature until his retirement in 1959 (just before Oxford University revised and improved its pension program, he said ruefully). It is interesting to note that although he garnered a rich array of academic honors, Tolkien never earned a degree beyond the baccalaureate.

He married Edith Bratt in 1916, and they had three sons and a daughter (to whom he wrote a delightful "Father Christmas" letter each year; these are now collected and published); he was a devout Roman Catholic in a country and an institution notable for anti-Catholic bias; he was a good friend of C. S. Lewis and other Oxonians of his day.

We can go back and see how any or all of this is relevant to *The Lord of the Rings.*

His date of birth: it is important to keep in mind that Tolkien was a grown man before World War I even began. His thought and sensibilities were products, to some extent, of late Victorian culture. They were formed in an age that was, if not more innocent than ours, then certainly more hopeful. Tolkien discounted most biographical data but thought it important to emphasize that "I was born in 1892 and lived . . . in 'the Shire' in a pre-mechanical age."[2]

The war experience: as Tolkien writes in the "Foreword" to *The Lord of the Rings:* "By 1918 all but one of my close friends were dead."[3] World War I exacted a terrible cost on Tolkien's generation, and there is a sense in which

The Lord of the Rings is an anti-war story, among the many other kinds of story it is. At the same time it is necessary to avoid, resist, and indeed combat purely allegorical readings of it: Mordor is not Nazi Germany, Tom Bombadil's little province is not Switzerland, and so on. Tolkien speaks of "applicability" (I, xi; *11*)—the behavior of evil is drearily alike in various times and places; all power struggles have some features in common.

The editing of the *OED* and the professorships: *The Lord of the Rings* is in a basic sense about language. The quality of one's language is a point of moral reference in the tale: Elvish is mellifluous and beautiful (it is meant to be, to our ears); Elves are good. Orkish is harsh and guttural; Orcs are evil. The relationship between great moral worth and beauty of speech is implicitly causal: the Elves have done and suffered much in the long ages of Middle-earth; they have acquired wisdom and nobility and poetry, and thus their languages have developed into instruments of great expressiveness. The Orcs, twisted creatures made in the dark, have no more intelligence than cunning amounts to, and are brutal and treacherous to boot; their grating tongue expresses these qualities.

The stories of Middle-earth began from love of language. Tolkien said, "The invention of language is the foundation. . . . To me a name comes first and the story follows."[4] For Tolkien, in the word was the beginning. It is well to consider how deep this goes; to invent an imaginary country or planet has its creative difficulties, to be sure, but to invent a language, with vocabulary, sounds, rules of grammar and syntax, and idiom, is a profound operation psychologically.

But that was Tolkien's métier: he had invented a couple of languages before he reached his teens, and during his career he invented at least a dozen others, based on or influenced by languages he had learned or was learning.[5] He knew at least four languages before he reached the British equivalent of high school.

This is a roster of the languages Tolkien knew or studied, besides Greek, Latin, Lombardic, and Gothic:

- among Germanic tongues: Old Norse or Old Icelandic; modern Swedish, Norwegian, and Danish; Old English or Anglo-Saxon; several dialects of Middle English; modern German and Dutch;

- among Romance languages: French, Spanish, Italian;
- in other language groups: modern and medieval Welsh, Russian, Finnish. (The two greatest influences on his development of Elvish languages were Welsh and Finnish.)

All these facts to the contrary notwithstanding, there is probably only limited usefulness in looking at the life to read the story, although Tolkien's relationship with C. S. Lewis should be mentioned. He and Tolkien were good friends for many years, even though they grew apart in the later years of Lewis's life. Tolkien always maintained that it was Lewis's faith in the worth of *The Lord of the Rings* and his insistence that Tolkien continue with it that led him eventually to complete the work.[6]

As a mature man, Tolkien was flagrantly ordinary: dowdy clothes except for the occasional brilliant waistcoat, plain food, a dull house, unremarkable pictures on the wall. In the ordinary acceptation of the terms, he had very little use for fashion or taste.

Everything was going on inside, in the imagination: he never cared to travel because he already had, so to speak. "One writes such a story [as *The Lord of the Rings*]," he said, "not out of the leaves of trees still to be observed . . . but it grows like a seed in the dark out of the leaf-mould of the mind, out of all that has been seen or thought or read, that has long ago been forgotten. . . ."[7]

Despite this diffidence, he was apparently a fascinating teacher: Anglo-Saxon is not the most glamorous of academic subjects, but one of his students, J. I. M. Stewart (Michael Innes), later wrote, "He could turn a lecture room into a mead hall, in which he was the bard and we were the feasting, listening guests."[8]

He was also a notable scholar; he wrote the pioneering criticism of the Old English poem *Beowulf,* in which he was one of the first to treat the poem as a work of art, and a highly wrought one at that, instead of as a gold mine for pedantic linguists. He edited with E. V. Gordon and others a number of medieval texts. And *The Lord of the Rings* is itself a highly literary text, as later remarks will suggest.

Still, he completed less work than he might have, for among his salient personality traits, he was both a procrastinator and a perfectionist. That is one reason why *The Lord of the Rings* took seventeen years to get itself written and published, and why *The Silmarillion* did not see print until after his death, when his son Christopher took it in hand, after Tolkien had been working on it for sixty years.

WHEN DID HOBBITS FIRST APPEAR?

Elves had figured in Tolkien's imaginative work from the outset. The Hobbits, by contrast, came rather late. They appeared in the late 1920s or early 1930s when Tolkien was correcting a very dull set of exam papers; distractedly, he wrote at the top of one, "in a hole in the ground there lived a hobbit."[9]

As he said, the name came first, then the story. He began to develop notions of what Hobbits were, what sort of a place they lived in, what adventures might be most surprising to them or one of them; the result was *The Hobbit,* published in 1937.

Tolkien, speaking of *The Hobbit,* always tried to correct two misconceptions:

It was not written *simply* for children, but it contained "'asides' to juvenile readers," as Tolkien's biographer Humphrey Carpenter calls them: Tolkien "came to dislike them, and even to believe that any deliberate talking down to children is a great mistake in a story."[10] Indeed, the condescension and preciosity that mar *The Hobbit* are largely absent from *The Lord of the Rings,* so he profited from the lesson. As Tolkien told another inquirer, if *The Hobbit* seemed "dressed up as 'for children,' in style or manner, I regret it. So do the children."[11]

Hobbits are not *little* people: they are not to be confused with the miniature elves and fays who hide in cowslips, nor with leprechauns, nor with any other race of beings whose essence is cuteness. They are indeed people; Tolkien's conception of them arises from his knowledge of country life. He said, "The Hobbits are just rustic English people, made small in size because it reflects the generally small reach of their imaginations—not the small reach of their courage or latent power."[12]

Although this study means to focus almost exclusively on *The Lord of the Rings,* a few words on its connection to *The Hobbit* may be appropriate here.

The continuity between the earlier and the later work is really rather slight. The Ring that Bilbo found or won under the mountain becomes the One Ring. The Hobbits themselves, and Gollum, and Gandalf, provide links; but the dissimilarities are more numerous than the similarities: the locales are different, most of the characters are different (in *The Lord of the Rings* the race of Dwarves has but two representatives), the realization of landscape and setting is vastly different. The nature of the plot is different: what happens to Bilbo in the earlier work is a series of discrete adventures; the fate of Frodo and the others in the later book is part of a single worldwide struggle.

Most of all, as what Tolkien said would suggest, the *tone* is different: there is more seriousness in *The Lord of the Rings*, there is more sense of moral implications. There is no sense of "playful intimacy" with imaginary children around an imaginary fireside.[13] Characters who appear in both books, like Gandalf, seem to have one less dimension (at least) in *The Hobbit*.

THE WRITING AND PUBLISHING HISTORY

As is true throughout Tolkien's created mythology, pieces of this tale existed from the earliest parts of his career; bits of *The Lord of the Rings* pre-dated Tolkien's conscious effort to tell a really long story. The success of *The Hobbit* for the Christmas season of 1937 led his publisher Allen and Unwin to encourage Tolkien to write a follow-up tale. The composition of *The Lord of the Rings* as such began soon after *The Hobbit* came out. Finally, seventeen years and 600,000 words later, it appeared in 1954 and 1955. It is *not* a trilogy, by the way, since that implies that each volume can stand alone, can be read separately and make sense. It is rather a long fiction in three volumes (which is the way novels by authors like Dickens were published in the nineteenth century). The three-volume format is a publisher's convenience: not only does it make the reader's task less unwieldy, it also assures three separate sets of reviews. After several chapters, beginning with "A Long-Expected Party" (all approved by young Rayner Unwin), it became clear that the story was changing direction. Humphrey Carpenter says, "Tolkien had not really wanted to write any more stories like *The Hobbit;* he had wanted to get on with the serious business of his mythology."[14]

At all events, the war, academic duties, career changes, and perhaps a sheer inability to see where the story was going (see Tolkien's remarks below) prevented his completing even a first draft until late 1947. Then the story had to be revised, "indeed largely rewritten backward" (I, ix; 9) and fair copied. Tolkien and the firm of Allen and Unwin also had had some misunderstandings; Tolkien let the firm of Collins read the typescript, but they eventually declined it, and Tolkien wound up back with Allen and Unwin. Rayner Unwin had always had faith in the story but it was clearly not going to be the juvenile best-seller that *The Hobbit* had been. The firm agreed to publish *The Lord of the Rings* as a kind of prestige item, believing it would sell a few thousand copies at best. Thus they made a financial arrangement rather unusual in modern publishing: instead of the usual royalty agreement where the author gets a percentage on every copy sold from the first on, usually 10 or 15 percent, Tolkien would get nothing until production costs were recovered—then he and the publisher would go 50–50.[15]

Some of the reasons that the writing process was so protracted have been mentioned; the process itself is of considerable interest. Tolkien speaks of the unfolding of the book not as if he were planning it, much less writing it, but as though it were happening to him. He writes, "the essential Quest started at once. But I met a lot of things on the way that astonished me." Tom Bombadil he knew of already, and he had heard rumor of the Mines of Moria, and of the Riders of Rohan. But Strider and the town of Bree, the Golden Wood of Lothlórien, and the Forest of Fangorn (among other things) were completely new. The strangest thing was that Saruman had not yet occurred to him and therefore he did not know why Gandalf had not shown up as promised![16]

And much more in the same vein. Authors often talk about their creations in this way, and to Tolkien's imagination, he was almost literally *in* Middle-earth.

At any rate, the book was well reviewed and enjoyed a modest reputation in England and America in hardcover until 1965, when the pirated Ace paperback edition appeared in the United States. Houghton Mifflin held the U.S. copyright to Tolkien's works, and court battles and lawsuits gained *The*

Lord of the Rings much valuable publicity, at which point—autumn 1965—Ballantine Books, by arrangement with Houghton Mifflin, put out the authorized paperback with authorial revisions.

A rapid growth in sales thereafter was both a result of the interest stirred by the legal warfare and a stimulus to further interest as word spread among readers. In the first ten months after the Ballantine paperback edition appeared, 250,000 copies were sold.

In the late 1960s Tolkien, his book, and its characters became cult figures on American campuses. "Frodo Lives!" buttons and graffiti were everywhere; the Tolkien Society was formed at Harvard; the *Tolkien Journal* began publication. There were maps and posters and calendars. By now of course, with millions of readers, *The Lord of the Rings* can no longer be regarded as a cult text, if the word "cult" means a small band of eccentric devotees. The influence of Tolkien's fantasy can perhaps be indicated by two rather obnoxious facts: it has spawned a host of (mostly meretricious) imitators, and it has become the subject of academic literary criticism.

Two

Geography, History, Theme

As its title suggests, this chapter proposes to draw closer to the elements of the text of *The Lord of the Rings,* taking up some general considerations before the succeeding chapters take up the text itself, book by book.

GEOGRAPHY

There is surprising variation among the several maps of Middle-earth (those of Tolkien himself, of his son Christopher Tolkien, of Pauline Baynes, for instance) but Middle-earth *seems* to extend about 1,200 miles from the Gulf of Lune (or Lhun) in the west to the Iron Hills in the east, and about 1,150 miles from the Ice Bay of Forochel in the north to Tolfalas at the Mouths of the Anduin in the south. Any map of course will show lands beyond these locations in three directions (to the west lies the Sea) but these regions do not enter into the action of the story. The 1,380,000 or so square miles as described above are the central arena of action.

There is a moral geography here as well: good flows from, and returns to, the West. Evil lurks in the East where its chief stronghold is; attack upon evil comes from the West.

One might reasonably ask, Middle-earth as middle of what?

In Old English poetry and in the old Teutonic cosmogonies with which Tolkien was familiar, "Middle-earth" ("middan-geard") was the name for the Earth itself, imagined as suspended between the sky above and the void below, or as poised spiritually between Heaven and Hell.

Considered as a flat land surface rather than vertically, Middle-earth can be thought of as lying between the ice of the North and the deserts of the South, or more importantly as between the loci of the forces of Good and Evil; it is their battleground:

Undying Lands   West/Númenor   Middle-earth   East

Given that so much that is important lies to the west of Middle-earth itself, and is frequently referred to by Men and Elves as both a source and a goal, a brief tour of proper names in this region might be useful to the reader, starting from the western shore of Middle-earth.

In the Sea west of Middle-earth was the great kingdom of Men, the island of Númenor or Westernesse. Tolkien's analogue of Atlantis, it was destroyed at the end of the Second Age. Faithful Númenoreans escaped to Middle-earth to found Arnor and Gondor and became the ancestors of Aragorn and Denethor and others of the noblest Men now alive.

Beyond Númenor is the island of Eressëa or Tol Eressëa, just off the eastern shore of the great land mass or continent called Aman. Aman is divided lengthwise by a mountain range. On the eastern side or shore—the mainland just opposite Eressëa—is Eldamar or Elvenhome (the Elvish and Westron names, respectively, for the land of the Elves): where they go when they leave Middle-earth, the land they love.

Beyond that mountain range, very far west, is Valinor, with its principal city, Valimar, the home of the Valar or "gods."

Beyond that is the end of the world.

Eressëa, Elvenhome/Eldamar, and Valinor are referred to collectively, and repeatedly, as "the West," "the Blessed Realm," "the Undying Lands," or "the Uttermost West" (this last term usually applying to Valinor alone).

Thus when Faramir, the Man of Gondor, recites his grace, he is being precise as to time and place when he says his people look toward "'Númenor that was, and beyond to Elvenhome that is, and to that which is beyond Elvenhome and will ever be.'" (II, 361; *336*) These places lie beyond Middle-earth historically, geographically, and spiritually, but how imaginary is Middle-earth itself?

Tolkien contends in his essay "On Fairy-Stories" that as God is creator so man is sub-creator; but there are limits to this creativity. A totally unrecognizable world, a totally strange one, would not only be impossible to create, but more to the point, it would be uninteresting or even repulsive.

"*Faërie*," says Tolkien, "contains many things besides elves and fays . . . or dragons: it holds . . . the earth and all things that are in it: tree and bird, water and stone . . . and ourselves, mortal men, when we are enchanted."[1] To visit the land of fantasy is not just to see new things; it is also to see familiar things in new ways.

Tolkien's literary pose in *The Lord of the Rings* is a standard one: that the subject matter is not his invention, but that he "is only a modern scholar who is compiling, editing, and eventually translating copies of very ancient documents of Middle-earth which have [somehow] come into his hands."[2] Thus he speaks of the personal records of the Hobbit heroes, of the Red Book of Westmarch, of documents in libraries in Rivendell and Minas Tirith; he invokes oral tradition, too, claiming that much wisdom and at least some information survives in the words of the folk.

All this is in the interest of establishing authenticity, all reasonable and familiar enough, but Tolkien goes further, identifying Middle-earth with our Earth long ago, and claiming (with a degree of whimsy, perhaps) that even now "Hobbits . . . linger . . . [in the] North-West of the Old World." (I, 21; *21*) That is, northwestern Europe and more specifically still, in terms of flora and fauna, if not of landforms, the British Isles. Yet the lands where, for instance, Treebeard used to wander are under the sea, due to the catastrophes that ended the First Age (see *The Silmarillion* and various other of Tolkien's writings for details). All the elf-kingdoms of the North, Beleriand, Nargothrond, Gondolin, Nogrod, Belagost, are gone. Only Lindon, of these old realms, remains above the Sea.

Exact locations in time or place are not a major concern; the land may be unfamiliar but the sky is not: our sun and moon are still there, although the sun is referred to as "she" and the moon as "he," the reverse of our nomenclature. The night sky is familiar: when Tolkien carefully describes "red Borgil" and Menelvagor "the Swordsman of the Sky," (I, 120; *111*) we are certainly looking at Mars and Orion. When the hobbits reach Bree we are told that the "Sickle* was swinging bright above the shoulders of Bree-hill" (I, 237; *217*), and the asterisk refers us to the foot of the page, where we learn that the Sickle is what the Hobbits call the Great Bear; that is, this constellation is explicitly identified with one in our sky, the one we more often call by still another name, the Big Dipper.

When we hear of Eärendil's Star (as we do at I, 261; *238* and 310–11; *284–5*) we know that it is Venus, for it is both the Evening and the Morning Star, and it is associated with a love story.[3]

The days, the nights, the seasons, are like ours in the Northern Hemisphere; these are all touches meant to show that Middle-earth could not possibly be some other planet, and meant to reassure readers that fundamentally they are on home territory, at least in a large sense. Details of plant and animal life, weather, skies, camping spots abound; again, this is not only a hallmark of Tolkien's individual style, but it also provides a kind of basing or grounding that allows the reader to swallow large doses of the marvelous.

These details also provide the basis for a recurrent pattern in the tale: the alternation of danger, then safety; or of misery, then comfort; sometimes of danger *and* misery, followed by safety *and* comfort:

- after the Old Forest, Tom Bombadil's house;
- after the Barrow-downs, Bree;
- after Weathertop, Rivendell;
- after Moria, Lothlórien, and so on.

HISTORY

Much of this material may be of ancillary interest to people who are reading *The Lord of the Rings* for the first time. The detail of historical data may be of secondary significance, but it grows on you over time, and will be revisited many times as we proceed through the story. Here I would like to lay out some of the ideas and concepts which shape *The Lord of the Rings,* as a guide to what to expect.

Two points appear at once:

The historical information (as given in Appendix B to Part III of *The Lord of the Rings* itself, for instance) tells us that we are coming into the story, not at the beginning, but rather near the end. That is, except for Chapter 1, we have a three-year view of a history which is demonstrably almost 7,000 years long, and uncountable years longer than that.

Because that is true, Tolkien can create an effect of great depth by reference and allusion. Middle-earth is rich in history because most of it has already taken place. Every locale seems to be a place where not only something is happening, but where something (or several things) happened long ago.

The depth of history as signaled by the succession of First, Second, and Third Ages is the historical corollary of Tolkien's great theme: the book is about the struggle of Good and Evil. Simple enough. But Tolkien sees the struggle as cyclical. Morally speaking, evil must always be vanquished, constantly re-arises, and must be vanquished again. The earliest plain statement of this is in Gandalf's words to Frodo: "'Always after a defeat and a respite, the Shadow takes another shape and grows again.'" (I, 81; *76*)

What Gandalf says immediately after this is of importance, too: Frodo has said that he wished it needn't have happened in his time, and Gandalf replies that we all wish that but such wishes are pointless: "'All we have to decide is what to do with the time that is given us.'" (I, 82; *76*). Thus Frodo and his friends are fated—how and by whom will be developed later—to participate in what is rapidly approaching.

Yet each age is not mere repetition: these are diminishing cycles: the First Age was greater than the Second (in both good and evil); the Second was greater than the Third (already in the Third Age, for instance, the Elves are leaving Middle-earth); the Third Age is greater than the Fourth Age-to-be (the Age of Men, as Tolkien calls it).

One example of the diminution from the Third to the Fourth Age is human longevity: the character Strider, the Ranger of the North whom Frodo and the others meet in the inn at Bree, looks to be about 35 or 40 years of age; weather-beaten to be sure, but hale, active, athletic, and so on. He is in fact when the hobbits meet him 87 years of age. He lives to be 210.

The second point, not to be lost amid all the history and the moral seriousness, is that this *is* a story—complete with a complex and carefully worked-out plot, a vast number and variety of characters, and terrific action. *The Lord of the Rings* lives at the level of adventure as well as anywhere else. Tolkien is a fine chronicler of battles, but he is even better at making you feel *danger;* few writers can equal him here. For example, when the hobbits are on their way out of the Shire, they detect someone or something following them, a great black entity on horseback, searching for something, sniffing for something (see I, 111, 116; *103, 107*). At least one reader of my acquaintance still gets a creepy feeling, goosebumps, when reading that, even though it may be for the two-dozenth time.

MORAL THEMES

The story is the chronicle of a struggle between Good and Evil, and they are frequently symbolized or represented by Light and Dark, in varying forms. It is Tolkien's privilege in a world of his making to choose what representations he will; he does not over-simplify things, although he may clarify things. Consider that Good is relatively weak and divided because it is free; Evil by contrast seems strong because its forces are united— though they may be in chains. But a turning point comes, very late. The tendency of Evil, because it is strong and composed partly of pride, is to over-reach and injure its own cause: *"oft evil will shall evil mar,"* is a truth stated often in the course of the tale (the wording cited here is at II, 255; *236*).

Evil struggles to gain power, Good to relinquish it. Thus the form of the book is a kind of inverted Quest, not to find something (the Fountain of Youth, Sleeping Beauty) but to lose or destroy something—the One Ring of evil Power.

The themes that accompany the idea of Quest are here: the journey itself, the unlooked-for help, the unexpected danger.[4] It is a Heroic Quest: the Fellowship of the Ring is formed at the Council of Elrond in Rivendell, and the company bravely sets forth from there southward. The Quest or journey thus started may obtain added significance from a detail found in "The Tale of Years" (Appendix B in Part III): the actual date on which they set out is December 25 (suggesting perhaps the seriousness of their undertaking, or perhaps goodwill and hope, and, with all of these, the idea of future sacrifice). The Nine travel south, are separated, and each member of the Company does the deeds it befalls him to do.

So the question to be explored given this separation might be, Who is a hero? And along with that, What is the nature of heroism in this tale? And can there be several varieties of heroism?

A collateral part of the action in *The Lord of the Rings* is to restore a king to his rightful throne, to restore a kingdom. How, one may reasonably ask, can the restoration of power be a subsidiary goal if the destruction of power is the chief goal? The answer may lie in making a meaningful distinction between power in itself and rightful authority. Tolkien's fantasy, like much fantasy, is instinctively and fundamentally conservative in its observance of—nay, insistence on—hierarchy and rightful rule.

Then, too, although the purpose is to conserve as much as possible, and to restore what can be restored, the destruction of evil is done at a great cost. Middle-earth will lose much that is good and beautiful as the evil is driven out. Everyone in the tale recognizes this—many comment on it; the tale is thus not particularly idyllic or optimistic.

Certain cultural considerations are worthy of special remark as one reads *The Lord of the Rings,* whether for the first or the tenth time.

What is the role of nature in the story? To what extent is it an active force or a living presence and not just scenery? How does it affect events? Does it have a moral dimension? Naturally (so to say) these are rhetorical questions: of course it has a moral dimension. One's closeness to and respect for nature is a measure of one's goodness, as distance from and disrespect for nature is a measure of evil.

What are the roles of women in the book? The number of female characters is limited, but are they therefore unimportant? Does Tolkien seem to have certain ideals of womanhood (and do those ideals have anything to do with his late Victorian upbringing)?

What about religion in the story? Tolkien was a deeply religious man, and faith was not the sort of thing he could simply omit from his imaginative life; but there are no churches, no sects, no clergymen in Middle-earth. Many other social institutions are represented; where is religion?

One might consider how each kind of character or group of characters contributes not only to the theme of the book (the struggle of Good and Evil, in broadest terms), but also to the feeling or flavor of the book: how much different or diminished the book would have been without Dwarves, or Riders of Rohan, or Rangers of Ithilien.

MYTHS AND LANGUAGE

Two other preliminary matters can be dealt with here before moving into the text itself: clearing up some identities by exploring, in greatly abridged form, Tolkien's creation myth and the early history of Middle-earth; and showing through several examples how some of Tolkien's linguistic resources have been deployed.

Middle-earth is the arena of action for Tolkien's story, but it is only part of the "world" that Tolkien imagined. As noted above, to the west of Middle-earth lie the blessed lands of Elves and gods, to which few others have access. To the east lie regions unknown. Tolkien set out his creation myth for his world in the early pages of *The Silmarillion;* here is a brief summary.[5]

Eru, the One, created a race called the Ainur, and in the music they made was created the world. Some of the Ainur entered physically into the world and became dwellers there. These entities were called the Valar by the Elves, and Tolkien notes that "Men have often called them gods." For the Elves, chief among the seven male and seven female Valar was Varda, Lady of the Stars, whom Elves in Middle-earth praise under the name Elbereth.

Tolkien's creation story combines some elements of the Christian and the pagan: as in Greek mythology, his "gods," the Valar, live in the physical world, if not among mortals; as the Greek gods supposedly lived on Mount Olympus, so the Valar live in the far West. Unlike their Greek counterparts they do not visit Middle-earth (or no longer do) but send messengers and helpers.

These helpers, like the Valar in kind but less powerful, are called Maiar, and among the greatest of them, it is said, was Olórin, friend and counselor to Men and Elves. When Faramir meets Frodo in Ithilien in Book IV, and describes a figure called the Grey Pilgrim, he notes that this individual goes by many names: Mithrandir, Incánus, and Olórin, among others. In the north of Middle-earth he is called Gandalf.

Thus Gandalf is one of the Maiar, acting for the Valar. According to Appendix B in Part III, about the year 1000 of the Third Age, five of the Maiar, called Istari or wizards, were sent (note passive voice) into Middle-earth. The two greatest of these were Gandalf and Saruman (III, 455; *417*); Saruman went often into the East, steeped himself in the lore of the Rings, and became corrupted. (We know of three wizards: Gandalf, known as the Grey; Saruman, called the White; and we hear of Radagast the Brown. But the other two are unaccounted for; it is one of the minor mysteries of the tale.)

Saruman the erstwhile White followed a pattern of corruption that had been laid out much earlier in Tolkien's history. As Lucifer in Christian myth fell and became Satan, so among the Valar one fell: Melkor fell into evil and total absorption in self and became Morgoth. And as Satan took many angels with him in his fall, so Morgoth took many of the Maiar, the greatest among whom was that spirit called Sauron.

Thus Gandalf and Sauron are of the same order of being, yet opposite: one fallen, the other unfallen. They are fitting and inevitable enemies, although in the course of the story they never in fact come into direct confrontation.

Gandalf's many names remind us once again of the primacy of language in this work. Its ground of being, Tolkien said, was "*fundamentally linguistic.*"[6] Although the common speech of Middle-earth is Westron, rendered in the text as English, you can see many examples of Tolkien's linguistic interests (particularly in Germanic tongues), and of the importance of language, just in some proper names:

- the wizard who went astray is Saruman; the Anglo-Saxon or Old English root "searu-" means "treachery" or "cunning"; thus, "man of treachery";
- the chief spirit of evil is Sauron; the Old Norse or Icelandic stem "saur-" supplies many words meaning "filth," or "dung," or "uncleanness";
- Gollum's name before he appropriated the Ring was Sméagol; the Old English word "smeagan" means "to ponder" or "to inquire"; related words give the sense of "creeping in" or "craftiness";

- his hapless cousin was Déagol, which is the Old English word for "hidden" or "secret";
- Théoden is the name of the King of Rohan; in Old English the world is a common noun meaning "chieftain" ("people-king");
- the giant female spider of Book IV is "Shelob"; Old English for spider is "lobbe";
- "ent" in Old English is "giant";
- "Mordor" derives from "morthor" which means "murder" in Old English; all the associations are negative: morbid, mortal, Modred of Arthurian legend;
- Théoden's horse is Snowmane, an easy derivation; Gandalf's horse, however, is "Shadowfax," from Old English "sceadu" meaning shadowy-gray, and "fax," "fæx," or "feax," meaning hair or coat (cf. Fairfax).

So in many cases Tolkien's professional work in languages provided him with proper names; his various invented languages were, as noted, strongly influenced by such tongues as Welsh and Finnish, which were among his linguistic hobbies.

Given the richness of language resources at Tolkien's disposal, it is not surprising (although it is maddening to some first-time readers) to find that many people, places, and things have two or more names. Elrond's home is Rivendell, a translation of Elvish Imladris, which translates again as Glen of the Cleft, all of which mean "split valley." Similarly, the man called Strider answers as well to his real name, Aragorn, and he is even more fully known as "Elessar, the Elfstone, Dúnadan, the heir of Isildur Elendil's son of Gondor." (II, 43; *42*) Late in the tale he takes the added name "Telcontar," which means Strider in High Elvish.

I said before that Tolkien created his world as a place where the languages he invented could be spoken; he put it more poetically and thus more tellingly by saying that he wrote *The Lord of the Rings* to create a world in which "Elen si la lumenn' omentielvo" would be a common greeting; it translates as "A star shines on the hour of our meeting." (I, 119; *110*)[7]

Three

The Fellowship
of the Ring:
Prologue and Book I

Significantly, Tolkien refers to the three separately bound pieces of his narrative not as volumes but as parts, thus further undercutting the notion of "trilogy." Thus Part I (which Tolkien also calls "the First Part"), *The Fellowship of the Ring,* contains Books I and II; Part II ("Second Part"), *The Two Towers,* contains Books III and IV; Part III ("Third Part"), *The Return of the King,* contains Books V and VI. The nomenclature can be confusing, especially with the use of Roman numerals for both divisions and sub-divisions, but the attentive reader will have little trouble.

Here is a general chronological outline of the Books:

- Part I, Book I begins shortly before September 22, 3001, Third Age (T. A.) and ends October 20, 3018, T. A.
- Part I, Book II begins October 24, 3018, and ends February 26, 3019, T. A.
- Part II, Book III begins February 26, 3019, and ends March 5, 3019, T. A.
- Part II, Book IV begins February 26, 3019, and ends March 13, 3019, T. A.

- Part III, Book V begins March 9, 3019, and ends March 25, 3019, T. A.
- Part III, Book VI begins March 14, 3019, and ends October 6, 3021, which is also the last year of the Third Age.

In Part I, Book I, we begin in normality, in the Shire, among those creatures of surpassing ordinariness called Hobbits. "I am in fact a hobbit," Tolkien once told a correspondent, "in all but size. . . . I smoke a pipe, [and] have a very simple sense of humor (which even my appreciative critics find tiresome). . . . I do not travel much."[1]

However Hobbit-like he thought himself, Tolkien clearly had far more than "the generally small reach of . . . imagination" that he attributed to his Hobbits (see p. 7 above). What he meant by that small reach is clear: Seeing a large black-clad figure on a black horse approaching his farmstead, Farmer Maggot wonders "what in the Shire" he can want. (I, 135; *125*) And Merry, sensing the presence of the same figure a little later, uses the same expression. Our idiom would be "What in the world is that?" To the Hobbits the Shire *is* the world.

At any rate, the race of Hobbits came westward into Eriador, founded the Shire, and began their count of years with 1 in the year 1601 of the Third Age. Since it is now (at the time of Chapter I, of Bilbo's party) 3001 T. A., it is 1401 in the Shire.

Among the Hobbits' odd traditions or habits is that of smoking pipes laden with tobacco, a custom they originated, and have passed on to many others, including Gandalf. Tolkien gave them this habit because he smoked a pipe, of course, but also we will see that pipe-weed is important later in the book. A principle can be stated here: (almost) nothing in this book is wasted.

Except for their love of genealogy, Hobbits have little sense of history; they have no sense that for a long time they have been both guarded by friends and watched by enemies. The first hint of trouble in and around the Shire comes with the increase in the number of Bounders, those who must guard the Shire's borders (see I, 31; *30*).

BILBO, FRODO, AND THE RING

After some general background about the divisions of the Shire (its far-things, or four parts), and the Shire's next-to-nonexistent government, we focus on two Hobbits, Bilbo and Frodo Baggins. Long ago, Bilbo had gotten a Ring—The Ring—from the creature Gollum, or perhaps the Ring got him: Tolkien tells us not that Bilbo put the Ring on but that "the Ring slipped quietly on to his finger." (I, 34; *32*) As Gandalf will shortly explain, the Ring has a way of acting in its own interest. The Ring is willful and perverse; its allegiance is to its maker, not its wearer—in a folkloric tradition, it might be called a Trickster figure.

Bilbo had the advantage of the Ring's conferral of invisibility and could have killed Gollum but "pity stayed him" (I, 34; *32*); he did keep the Ring, though. "Pity" will be important at every encounter with a figure like Gollum, at once forlorn and malicious.

So Bilbo returned to the Shire eventually, and eventually he adopted his kinsman Frodo, whose parents had accidentally drowned. In what degree kinsman? Gaffer Gamgee is right when he explains that Frodo is Bilbo's "first *and* second cousin, once removed either way" (I, 45; *43*), as a glance at the family trees in Appendix C (III, 473–7; *434–8*) will show. But in terms of the quality of the relationship, the difference in age, and their feelings toward each other, Tolkien is surely right to overlook his own technicality and call Bilbo and Frodo uncle and nephew, as he does at least twice. (I, 32; *30;* I, 297; *272*) It is at any rate characteristic of some kinds of tales to involve an uncle-nephew relationship; there can be seniority in the relation but also an equality impossible with father and son. Such a pairing also does away with the need for a household and such appurtenances as mother, siblings, etc.

Bilbo and Frodo are different from most other Hobbits:

- both are bachelors in a Hobbit-culture very much oriented to family and children (for the same convenience as just mentioned: they have no family obligations, are free to travel, and so on);
- both are rich;

- both are friends with Elves;
- both *do* travel.

In the Shire it is quite unusual for any Hobbit to go much farther than Bree, and as the days have been darkening few go even that far. Like the English peasantry of earlier centuries, Hobbits are most likely to live and die within a few miles of their birthplace. And many Hobbits are truculently xenophobic.

In the first chapter of Book I, what strikes one as significant is the *tone*: it is not the child-talk or condescending jollity of *The Hobbit*, but it certainly is lighter in tone than later chapters; it is cheerful; the speaker is clearly enjoying himself. Perhaps this tone has a purpose: to ease us into the world of Middle-earth by way of the unpretentious and domestic realm of the Shire, making us comfortable there before the adventures begin.

More significantly perhaps, this tone suggests that Tolkien began the tale as what his publishers wanted: a sequel to *The Hobbit*. The parallel of chapter titles—in *The Hobbit* "An Unexpected Party," here "A Long-Expected Party"—is certainly no accident. But as has been suggested already, the direction which *The Lord of the Rings* soon began to take was anything but parallel to *The Hobbit*.

There is more broad humor in this chapter than anywhere else in the tale; later humor tends to be more along the lines of "grim jest" than "rustic joke" (as, for instance, the running banter between Gimli the Dwarf and Éomer of Rohan about the beauty of the Lady Galadriel). At any rate, the upshot of the chapter, and the windup of the party, is that Bilbo goes away as planned and is constrained, at the cost of some erosion of his and Gandalf's friendship, to leave his Ring behind. In spite of his reluctance, he is the first person ever to give up the Ring voluntarily, as Gandalf observes. (I, 87; *81*)

What are the powers and attributes of this One Ring, at once the result of great evil and the cause of much more?

- it can make trouble between friends, as Bilbo's behavior suggests;
- it can make you invisible: this saved Bilbo's life beneath the mountain, and it has since saved him a good deal of what he might call

"botheration" whenever someone like Lobelia Sackville-Baggins comes into view;

- it can stretch out your life span: it does not make you live longer in the fullest sense; rather the Ring seems to take what life force or energy you have and stretch it over a longer period of time, so that you begin to look thinned or attenuated after a while;
- the Ring can give you power according to your stature (I, 85; *79*): Sméagol or Gollum, its former keeper, was a sneaky unpleasant thing before he came into possession of the Ring; the Ring just enhanced those qualities. Gandalf, for example, knows something about his own stature and nature, and knows that the Ring would make him very powerful and would corrupt him eventually. He consistently refuses it.

For this plain gold Ring is beautiful and desirable, and altogether evil. As Gandalf tells Frodo, Sauron "'let a great part of his . . . power pass into it. . . .'" (I, 82; *76*) And Sauron of course wants it back; it would give him worldwide rule.

The Ring is powerful in itself: one of the underlying ironies of the tale is that whoever thinks he possesses the Ring is in fact possessed by it. It had to a degree enslaved Gollum; he was mostly in its power. And this is the plight of one who never even *used* the Ring in any significant way, but only kept it and hid it.

Here we learn for the first time that there is more than one set of unseen forces at work. That Bilbo found the Ring is not quite the right way to put it; rather, according to Gandalf, the Ring left Gollum: forces were at work, Gandalf suggests, over which Sauron had no power, thus "'Bilbo was *meant* to find the Ring, and *not* by its maker. In which case you [Frodo] also were meant to have it.'" (I, 88; *81*)

The reader naturally asks, Who meant Bilbo to find the Ring? That answer emerges only gradually and over a long period of time. Deep and conflicting currents are moving under the story's surface, as we now begin to sense.

The Ring sits atop a hierarchy of rings. Gandalf had earlier tested it in Frodo's fireplace and the fire revealed the fine characters inscribed inside and outside its circle. The characters are Elvish, but the language of the inscription is the Black Speech of Mordor; Gandalf refuses to utter the words of that language (although he does speak them later at the Council of Elrond [I, 333; *305*]), but translates the words on the Ring into the Common Speech:

One Ring to rule them all, One Ring to find them,
One Ring to bring them all and in the darkness bind them. (I, 81; *75*)

Won over by Sauron and under his influence, the Elven-smiths of the Second Age had made the Three Rings, the Seven, and the Nine, and they were given to Elves, Dwarves, and Men respectively. Sauron then undertook to craft the One Ring himself to rule all the others. The Nine of course went to those mortal kings who as the Black Riders (Ringwraiths or Nazgûl) became Sauron's servants. Four of the seven Dwarf Rings were consumed by dragons; the other three Sauron recovered himself.

But where are the Three Rings of the Elves? Why did they not suffer the fate of the Seven and the Nine? The relationship of the Three Elven Rings to Sauron is not altogether clear. It is suggested that the great Elven leader Celebrimbor foresaw what Sauron was up to and hid the Rings from him. (I, 82, 318, 332; *76; 292; 304*) Yet Elrond says that when the One Ring passed out of all knowledge, the Three were released from its dominion (I, 321; *295*); this is not quite the same as saying that Sauron never had anything to do with them. And again, the statement (I, 352; *322*) that if Sauron regains the One he will have power over the Three does not seem consistent with what is said elsewhere. And in the same place it is suggested that if the One is destroyed the Three might go free or alternatively might lose all their power.

At this early point in the narrative, however, much remains unclear; we may have to await the actual fate of the One Ring to learn the truth about the Three.

GANDALF

We learn some interesting things about Gandalf the Grey in these early pages; we learn, for instance, that he had made a mistake in letting Gollum go years earlier. (I, 91; *84*) There are real limitations on Gandalf's powers, but it is fascinating to watch them being gradually revealed even before his fall in Moria and his return as the White. Already there is a hint in his stern admonitions to Bilbo to leave behind the Ring, and much more will appear in Book II. To the Hobbits he has been just a wise old man with a flair for fireworks displays; who and what he really is the Hobbits will learn, sometimes to their discomfiture.

Gandalf is certainly one of the most celebrated characters in all of Tolkien's Middle-earth gallery. In these early pages it is not yet apparent that he is also one of the most complex: he can be avuncular, he can be crotchety. He can be warm, or remote. His patience is tried, and his wisdom ignored, by the less intelligent of his companions (that is, by most of them). He was sent, he tells us later, to do his work in Middle-earth, but we see eventually that he is there because he loves the place and its inhabitants, whether dense Men, stubborn Dwarves, or foolish Hobbits. In his human form, Gandalf represents some of the highest human traits, not least of them courage, foresight, and self-sacrifice.

FRODO'S JOURNEY BEGINS

At all events, Frodo leaves the Shire as scheduled in late September, but he is much concerned about Gandalf's untoward absence. He leaves, accompanied by his two kinsmen, Meriadoc Brandybuck and Peregrin Took (Merry and Pippin), and by his servant Sam Gamgee. He leaves, but finds himself followed by a strange horseman (who apparently can smell and hear but cannot see very well); the strange horseman reappears that evening. (I, 111, 116; *103, 107*)

Here is established a basic pattern of happenings. To generalize: the rider is there (danger), Frodo desires urgently to put on the Ring (mistake or carelessness), Elves come singing through the woods (unlooked-for help). A similar pattern, with variants, occurs twice when the hobbits meet Tom Bombadil, first when he rescues them from Old Man Willow, and second when he frees them from the Barrow-wights.

Yet again, in *The Prancing Pony* at Bree: Frodo puts on the Ring in the taproom (I, 219; *201*), two men slip out (to notify the Nazgûl, presumably),

Strider comes forward as a friend; here the pattern is mistake, danger, help. A similar sequence of events takes place at Weathertop and at the Ford of Bruinen at the very end of Book I.

The pattern can be extended still further: in each case, when unlooked-for help arrives there is a conference, or counsel is taken, often in the presence of food and drink. The result is a movement of the Ring, and the movement involves or provokes the next sequence of mistake, danger, help.[2]

Help is not always from the outside: at Weathertop it is Frodo's own courage or strength of mind—unexpected though it is—that, along with the aid of language, saves the day. At the crucial moment Frodo cries, "*O Elbereth! Gilthoniel!*" Hateful to the ears of the Black Riders is the language of the Elves: as Strider later tells Frodo, "'More deadly [than a blade] was the name of Elbereth.'" (I, 265; *243*)

To go back just a bit: we know that these Black Riders—Ringwraiths—Nazgûl (the word "nazg" means "ring" in the Black Speech of Mordor) are the nine mortal men, great kings of old, to whom Sauron gave the Nine Rings and thereby ensorcelled them.

They have certain sensory capacities and limitations, as Strider explains: "'They themselves do not see the world of light as we do'" (I, 255–6; *234*), but they have extraordinary senses, enhanced by the Ring's evil.

The love of darkness, the desire for blood: these things make the Nazgûl seem much like vampires. Tolkien does not develop what may be only a passing resemblance (to make an explicit comparison would only be to vulgarize the image of the Riders), but clearly these wraiths desire Frodo's soul, perhaps as much as their master desires Frodo's Ring.

They produce their effects (usually of terror) simply by being what they are and by being in the vicinity; as servants of the Ring-maker the Ring draws them, as Aragorn noted, but also their mere proximity makes Frodo want to put on the Ring. They also give forth a kind of exhalation or exudation that is to a degree poisonous or noxious; "the Black Breath," Strider calls it, and Merry is affected by it in Bree; he is found in the Road in a hagridden sleep. (I, 236; *216*)

Just as the One Ring confers invisibility on its wearer, we may suppose that the Nine Rings, similarly crafted after all, are what make the Nazgûl invisible. But they cannot see mortals either, in the ordinary way; their advantage is also their limitation. They hover on the borders of sight (seeing or being seen) in a strange and twilit existence, and their inability to see can be a moral as well as a physical disadvantage.

Almost two weeks from Weathertop to Rivendell, Frodo wounded, the Ringwraiths out there somewhere, the Road unsafe; it will begin to seem like a very long fortnight indeed. The cheerless countryside the party passes through and the miserable dispiriting weather are mirrors of Frodo's pain and the peril of their journey. There is little in this last chapter of Book I in the way of plot development except that when they meet Glorfindel the Elf, they learn that he is abroad searching for them or for signs of the Black Riders because of messages sent by the Elves whom Frodo and the others met back in the Shire. (I, 116–24; *107–13*) The misery of the party's journey is relieved only by this meeting and by Sam's song about the trolls.

TOM BOMBADIL

It is easy to overlook the various excellences of Book I, possibly because, in it, the plot has not thickened enough—with only one line of events in train, it is hard to see how events are going to relate or conflict.

Still, at this point, there have already been examples of unexpected dangers: the Black Riders, Old Man Willow (who exhibits a hostility or malice in the world of nature not necessarily connected with the evil of Sauron or the Ring), the Barrow-wights. And there have been examples of unlooked-for help: the first meeting with the Elves, Farmer Maggot, Tom Bombadil.

Who is Tom Bombadil? Who is this creature bounding about the woodlands in blue coat and yellow boots, singing to himself? When Frodo asks that question, Tom's helpmate Goldberry replies, "'He is the Master of wood, water, and hill'" (I, 174; *160*), and goes on to say that nothing belongs to Tom; all that of which he is master belongs to itself. Tom's mastery consists of seeing to it that all in his realm preserves its own identity—is, in a word, free.

Thus Tom can be considered a kind of nature spirit, or, since he was in Middle-earth before the forms of nature itself, he can be thought of as a kind of ground for nature's being. He may be a Vala, he may be a Maia, or he may be *sui generis*.

In Tolkien's conception, this figure existed well before either *The Hobbit* or *The Lord of the Rings*. Tolkien had written poetry about him in *The Oxford Magazine* in 1933 and 1934. In December 1937, before incorporating Tom into *The Lord of the Rings,* Tolkien identified him as "the spirit of the (vanishing) Oxford and Berkshire countryside."[3]

Later, Tolkien identified Tom, or at least his function, more fully; he put Tom in as an enigma "intentionally," he told the novelist Naomi Mitchison, and "as a comment." He went on, "I do not really write like that," half apologizing for the hearty jolly-fellow presentation of Tom. Tom represents a position, both disinterested and uninterested, in the political struggle for power between Good and Evil. Unlike Tom, says Tolkien, "Both sides in some degree, conservative or destructive, want a measure of control." Tom as a natural force of sorts does not take sides, but he needs Good to win in order to survive, whether he acknowledges it or not. Tom might survive longer than other entities, but in Sauron's world he would succumb at last.[4]

So Tom Bombadil represents a point of view which prefers the neutral and the pacific. He is not affected by the Ring (he puts it on and does not disappear, Frodo puts it on and Tom can still see him), because he is completely outside or beyond the power struggle of which the Ring is the focus, as well of course as being antecedent to the Ring in time. Yet Tolkien is also right in saying that Tom needs the Free Peoples. The very fact that Tom Bombadil is on the side of life and freedom means that he is on the side of the West, almost by definition. And Tom may seem almost silly at first, but like Strider a few days later at Bree, he will turn out to be a different and subtler being than a first impression might indicate. (For more about Tom and the odd power of his realm, see Chapter 16 below.)

Tom rescues the hobbits from the terrors of the Barrow-downs and their evil denizens, the Barrow-wights. Two separate layers of history are represented in the Barrow-downs, both encapsulated in Tom's talk: kings fought and died there; later, evil "'Barrow-wights walked in the hollow places. . . . '" (I, 180–1; *167–8*)

The weapons found there (short swords and the like, which Tom gives to the hobbits) were wrought by the enemies of Evil—specifically the enemies of the Witch-King of Angmar, who was defeated, and fled, and assumed leadership of the Nazgûl. So these are weapons of Good, and will be important later.

The importance of the episode on the Barrow-downs lies in the future use of these ancient weapons, and also in the appearance of early signs of Hobbit courage. Frodo regains consciousness in the barrow, paralyzed by fear, but, Tolkien says, "There is a seed of courage hidden . . . in the heart of the fattest and most timid hobbit. . . ." (I, 194; *178*) Frodo is neither very fat nor very timid, but in this moment his seed of courage takes root and he is able to act with bravery and dispatch.

All that stands between the hobbits' escape from the Barrow-downs and the attack on Frodo at Weathertop is the sojourn at *The Prancing Pony* in Bree. The principle of contrast operates here, of course, as the hobbits find food and shelter after the cold and fog and fear of the Barrow-downs. The news in Gandalf's never-delivered letter—that Frodo should leave the Shire by late July at the latest—only reinforces our sense that in the hobbits' attempt to get to Rivendell too little is happening too late. Countervailing this is the sense that in the hitherto unmet Strider the hobbits will be finding a friend and a strong ally.

But it is not unfair to say that the unspoken theme of Book I is discouragement, by which I mean that the reader can easily become more discouraged than the characters. There is the sense—and we sense it long before Gandalf's letter makes it plain—that everything has been left too late, and that the forces of evil have gained far too much strength and momentum. Everything seems to be pushing the hobbits into the worst possible situation at every turn, as, for instance, the very terrain of the Old Forest seems to be directing them inexorably toward Old Man Willow. Everything that happens seems to militate against the possibility that Frodo and his friends can succeed even in the modest goals of getting out of the Shire, of reaching Bree, of coming at last to Rivendell.

Four

THE FELLOWSHIP OF THE RING: BOOK II

Among the six books of Tolkien's story, Book II is outstanding because it is the most varied. We go from mountaintops to mines deep in the earth; we go from the darkness and bloodshed of Moria to the peace and golden light of Lothlórien. The testing of Frodo and the other hobbits, begun in Book I, continues as we pass from one Elven stronghold to another, and on down the great river. The powers of Gandalf begin to appear at their fullest, and much of Gandalf's power is in language; words have magic. Still, this is a book of losses, that of Gandalf himself not least; and here we both meet and lose Boromir. In fact it is only within this one book that the Fellowship of the Ring exists at all: it is unformed when the book opens and broken when it closes.

The first two chapters of Book II, in particular, can summon up some of the feeling that lies beneath *The Lord of the Rings*. "Many Meetings" suggests both the reunion of old acquaintances and the first greetings among strangers, both in an effort to defeat evil; "The Council of Elrond" is a background chapter in which we and those taking counsel gain much information about the evil nature and the history of the Ring; almost everyone present has something to contribute to that story as they move toward the decisions that must be made. (As a fairly obvious literary device, "Many

Meetings" here is to be set against "Many Partings" in Book VI when the Quest is done.)

That first chapter gives us even deeper background, in a way: on what might be called the home lives of the Elves. We meet more Elves in Book II than anywhere else in Tolkien's tale, and here at Rivendell we see the comfortable excellence of their lives. They dwell in a world of physical ease and cultural splendor. Song, music, and story are part of their daily existence, we gather, and yet the Elves are mindful that this too shall pass away. Elves had chosen to live in Middle-earth because they loved it, and their lives and institutions there seemed durable. Now they must face the recognition that their tenure in this realm is to be short.

Tolkien has perhaps placed these chapters at the opening of Book II—the beginning of the Fellowship's actual quest or journey—not only because they are necessary in terms of narrative understanding, but also because they bring home in several ways how much is at stake in the journey.

That is somewhat in the future, but the opening pages of Book II constitute a sort of book of revelations for Frodo as he recovers from his knife wound. He is in the Last Homely House East of the Sea in its last days in the life of Middle-earth. He is there in the last hours, so to speak, of Elves' presence in Middle-earth, and he sees Arwen, daughter of Master Elrond: she is the last of three Elven women who must choose marriage, mortality, and Middle-earth. Frodo sees old Bilbo, who will play an indirect but unexpectedly crucial role in the adventures to come.

Among many surprises, Frodo is most surprised to learn the real status and identity of the Man who has accompanied him from Bree through many perils. Frodo may be quite cosmopolitan among Hobbits, but even his perspectives must widen somewhat in the great outer world. Aragorn is not a "mere" Ranger, as Frodo had thought: Gandalf tells Frodo that the Rangers are in fact the last of the Men of the West, of Númenor, which was destroyed at the end of the Second Age.

The Appendices trace Aragorn's heritage back in fact to the line of the kings of Númenor, the first of whom was Elros the brother of Elrond. Elrond chose to be an Elf, therefore immortal, and lives in Rivendell. Elros had chosen to be human, therefore mortal, and lived in Númenor.

Thus the early pages of Book II imply, without quite explicitly stating, two themes or threads that run throughout the story: the bittersweet fate of the Elves no matter how the Ring is disposed of, and the ages-long hunger of the mortal for immortality. We will see more of these themes as the tale proceeds.

Frodo certainly senses how much beauty the world and the culture of the Elves contains. The Elves are the height of what human beings might be, and their relation to the world of nature and of society is one of harmony and wisdom. "Fair," "noble," "wise," and "sad" are words we hear used of the Elves time and time again. Their languages are lovely (at least Tolkien designed them so), their music ethereal, and their architecture at once gracefully proportioned and made for Elven and human use.

Frodo regrets having to leave the Elves' singing even for a good chat with Bilbo. He stands enchanted as a song begins:

A Elbereth Gilthoniel
silivren penna míriel
o menel aglar elenath!
(see I, 312; *286* for full text)

These words open a song of praise to the Vala, Varda, known on this side of the Sea as Elbereth, the tutelary spirit of the Elves. The words of praise, in what can be called a very free translation, are found in the song that the Elf Gildor and his companions are singing when Frodo meets them in the Shire. (I, 117; *108*)

Without being ostentatiously religious, the Elves are a people of reverence: they are looked up to by their fellow-dwellers in Middle-earth, and they in turn revere the powers beyond the Sea who have been their patrons and protectors. Thus there is a hymnodic quality and power to their verse (as seen here and in the "Farewell to Lórien" near the end of Book II), which contrasts vividly with, say, the songs of the Hobbits. Hobbit music, or Hobbit lyrics anyway—we know little of the tunes—live in the everyday world. Depending on the specific selection, you can hear in it popular or folk songs, children's songs, and even echoes from English music halls and comic theater.

THE COUNCIL OF ELROND

Singing and feasting are appropriate to celebrate the many meetings at Rivendell, but the main business at hand is the Council of Elrond. Many commentators have called Tolkien's fiction an epic (although he himself did not) and certainly in the general sense it is epic in sweep and scope. But it also shares with literary epic such features as the scene of counsel here.

Tolkien naturally uses the traditional device for his own purposes. In most of the epic councils that come readily to mind, the meeting is held between a leader and his lieutenants or allies (as Agamemnon and the other Greek leaders in their tents before Troy), or it is held in order to bring about a predetermined result (as the clever stage-management of Satan and Beëlzebub at the Council in Pandemonium in *Paradise Lost*). Neither of these things is true of the Council of Elrond. Boromir, a Man of Gondor far to the south, is a stranger in Rivendell; hardly less out of place are the Dwarf Glóin and his son Gimli, or Legolas the Wood-Elf, to say nothing of Frodo and the wonderstruck hobbits who have accompanied him. Most of those at the Council are meeting to find out, among other things, why they are there.

And although Elrond himself and Gandalf have the greatest foresight and wisdom of all those present, they do not have a preset goal or plan of action in mind. The whole course of discussion suggests that they can foresee what may have to happen, but the Council of Elrond is a gathering where, to some degree or other, all have much to learn. Each participant brings a particular perspective from his own corner of Middle-earth.

The functions of the Council of Elrond, for the characters and for the reader, are several:

- to show that all the troubles of Middle-earth are of a piece. As each participant brings information, so each, like Glóin the Dwarf, is informed that his situation is part of a greater and more dangerous situation;
- to determine, and show to all present, that the ring Frodo has brought is the One Ring of Power, as Gandalf and Elrond explain at length the history and identity of this lovely circlet of plain gold;

- to return Gollum to our awareness, as Legolas ruefully explains that the miserable creature has escaped the custody of the Wood-Elves. When Gandalf hears this he resignedly makes what will turn out to be a key statement: Gollum "'must do what he will. But he may play a part yet that neither he nor Sauron has foreseen.'" (I, 336; *307*);
- to learn from Gandalf (as we do) why Saruman, Gandalf's brother wizard, who knows more Ringlore than anyone else in Middle-earth, is not here. He has turned traitor. Having lured Gandalf to his fortress of Orthanc, Saruman preaches counsels of expediency: the end, he says, justifies the means amid the shifting powers at war within Middle-earth. Gandalf rejects these counsels, but the point seems to be that Saruman is failing in self-knowledge: a renowned orator, he has traded his robes of white for a robe of many colors. In imitation of, or tribute to, Sauron, he wears a ring.

When Gandalf relates how he strode back and forth on the pinnacle of Orthanc, Frodo exclaims, "'I saw you!'" and explains to the astonished Gandalf, "'It was only a dream. . . . '" (I, 342; *313*) It was a dream that Frodo had had in the house of Tom Bombadil, that site of strange dreams and strange events. Gandalf goes on to speak of his great horse Shadowfax, untiring, speedy, beautiful. The love between horse and wizard is a concrete example of moral worth as measured by closeness to, or distance from, the world of nature. Men and others can be judged by the horses they keep and how well they keep them.

The Council of Elrond must also decide, as one of its chief functions, what to do with the Ring. What are its choices?

- to send it to some neutral party like Tom Bombadil? No: even if one could get it back there, Tom has no regard for the Ring—he might as readily throw it away as safeguard it;
- to send it right out of Middle-earth? No: the problem must be solved here;
- to drop it in the Sea? No: even that does not make it safe forever (it came out of the water to Sméagol after all);

• to use it? This notion is the one contribution of Boromir to the discussion, a wrong-headed one that shows he does not understand the purity and malignity of the Ring's evil.

The choices seem to narrow down to: hide the Ring, or unmake it. "Choice" is a significant word in this book of *The Lord of the Rings* as in many other parts. Choices are limited by external circumstance, and also by the nature of the choosers. The first limitation always seems to make the choices harder and more dangerous; the second limitation brings out character and moral and intellectual stature in the face of that danger and hardship. Frodo and Aragorn and others do not worry about questions of free will vs. necessity, or other philosophical parameters of "choice"; they operate by standards of love, and loyalty, and duty, and selflessness, and other ideas whose names they might blush to hear.

To hide the Ring is only to delay making a choice; the Ring must be unmade, and to unmake the Ring one must take it to Sauron's very doorstep; yet, observes one council member, that is a foolhardy notion that will lead to despair.

Gandalf's reply to this objection is worth keeping in mind throughout the rest of the story: "'despair is only for those who see the end beyond all doubt.'" (I, 352; *322*) We will see in later chapters what happens when despair prevails: to give up seems often enough the logical or the rational thing to do, but never is it the wise thing to do. Despair, as Gandalf's remark implies, arises from pride and a feeling of omniscience, and too often in the tale, as Gandalf will have occasion to mention again, sentient creatures suffer from an excess of both. From a linguistic point of view alone, "despair" is one of those resonant words, like "pity" (or "choice"), that informs the behavior of characters and shapes the course of the narrative.

What Gandalf goes on to say—that Sauron can judge the motives of others only by his own—is worth noting too: it suggests the basic defect or weakness of evil—evil lacks imagination.[1] Evil is so wrapped up in self that it cannot conceive how another mind might work, or what another person might think. The great literary model for evil, Milton's Satan, is such an egoist that even awakening on the burning floor of Hell, he starts talking about himself within ten lines. And he cannot imagine that the motives which actuate him—revenge, power-seeking—do not actuate God.[2] Likewise, according to Gandalf's acute understanding of his adversary, Sauron's moral and thus psychological blindness can provide a path, faint though it may be, direct to the destruction of the Ring.

And so the decision is made to destroy the Ring, which can only be done at Mount Doom in Mordor, the place of its making. Then the question arises: Whom to send? All present gently dissuade Bilbo from getting up immediately and marching eastward, which he offers to do. Then in spite of his yearning for peace and repose, Frodo speaks *as if some other will was using his small voice.* 'I will take the Ring,' . . . 'though I do not know the way.'" (I, 354; *324;* emphasis added)

And Elrond responds that no one is likely to know the way, if Frodo does not; it is his duty.

Thus the questions of what to do, and who shall do it, both seemingly rich in possible answers, come down to only one answer each. In spite of the phraseology of "some other will," the choice is Frodo's and the choice is Frodo. As Elrond goes on to suggest, the Hobbit race is now coming into its own. The wisdom of Gandalf, the appointee of the Valar, in interesting himself in the affairs of Hobbits now becomes plain. Hobbits come to the fore. A Hobbit is far from an obvious choice to undertake this momentous errand, but to send a Hobbit to Mordor makes sense strategically. Small, insignificant, unlikely, a Hobbit might be overlooked for a time. And all that has happened to Frodo since he left the Shire (just over a month ago!), all the testing of his courage and coolness, makes the choice of *this* Hobbit morally the best.

SOUTHWARD

When the Council of Elrond adjourns, messengers are sent forth to scout out the lay of the land, and weapons are prepared and refurbished. Elrond chooses the Company of Nine Walkers to answer the Nine Riders of Mordor, and Merry and Pippin are included, on Gandalf's advice and against Elrond's better judgment: an interesting pair of selections.

As the Company heads south, we sense more strongly than ever how empty Middle-earth has become. Already at Bree we had learned that the old

North Road, once a busy road for travelers, is now little used and grown with grass. Here, as the Company travels south on the western side of the Misty Mountains, they pass through great stretches of empty land: "'no folk dwell here now," observes Aragorn, and Legolas says that the Elves who formerly lived here have long ago sought the Grey Havens and passed West over Sea.

Decreasing population is part of the general sense of decline throughout Middle-earth: the banks of the River Anduin are empty of people; empty lands stretch between Isengard and the Shire, Aragorn notes later. Folk have departed Middle-earth for more congenial places, as the Elves are doing; or have suffered their numbers to decrease, as the Dwarves have. Some folk have simply given up: children are among the rarest things in Middle-earth, except perhaps in the Shire. Sauron's evil can be defined as the hatred of life, especially free life not under his tyranny; the emptiness of the lands (while he may not have directly caused it) is both a triumph for his power and a symptom of his evil. On a merely practical level, the emptiness of the lands of Middle-earth plays into Sauron's hands, too. It leads to xenophobia and distrust among those populations that remain. They seldom travel any more, they seldom speak as one group to another, they lack information or they get information only in the form of rumor and ill-report. Mutual suspicion is the keynote of relations among the dwindling numbers in the ever more silent countryside, a situation that must create malicious glee in the dark hearts of Mordor.

The Company must in any case get to the other side of the Misty Mountains: the way around their southern end would take the travelers into the enemy territory of Saruman; the way over the top is barred by weather (to keep them all from freezing as they vainly attempt the heights of Mount Caradhas Gandalf has to use his magic to start a fire, and thus he unmistakably reveals his whereabouts to any interested observer in that part of Middle-earth).

We get the sense again that where choices had seemed to exist, they do not. The Company must go under the mountains through the Mines of Moria. That is the hardest choice, because it is the most dangerous and dreaded route. But it is the only choice left. The Nine must take their courage in both hands and walk in.

FROM DARK TO LIGHT:
MORIA TO LOTHLÓRIEN

Merely to pass the Doors into the Mines of Moria is easy enough; they are a monument to a simpler and more innocent age: all you need do to get in is say "Friend" in Elvish ("Mellon"). But having once entered, why is Gandalf especially at risk? The answer eventually comes in the wizard's confrontation with the fire-creature the Balrog. It like him is a Maia; they are equal and opposite forces in a deadly duel.

That meeting comes at the end of a journey during which Tolkien again makes you feel danger in the highest degree. Everything has already conspired to force the Company to this location; everything in the surroundings seems not only watchful but hostile: the stream at the Doors is not where it is supposed to be, the way is not clear, and a threatening evening is coming on. Peril is impending even as the party reaches the Doors, and from then on the sense of the terrible increases: the Watcher in the pool before they even enter the Mines; the winds from various side passages; the holes, chasms, and pitfalls at every step; the halts to ascertain direction; the noises, including the noise Frodo hears or imagines he hears like faint footsteps behind them; the chamber where they learn the fate of the Dwarves who had returned to Moria some thirty years ago; and finally the confrontation with Orcs in which Frodo seems to be seriously wounded.

Yet after escaping the perils of Moria, the Company comes to the Golden Wood of Lothlórien, ruled by the Lady Galadriel and her spouse/escort Celeborn. Rivendell and Lothlórien are the two major Elvish strongholds left in this part of Middle-earth. But the contrast between them is enormous. Rivendell is a house, actually—a kind of great lodge; Lothlórien is a country. Rivendell is a kind of crossroads or is at least a meeting-place, as we have seen; many were welcome there in former days. Lothlórien is secret, unvisited, closely guarded; so secluded that later the Riders of Rohan say they believe it is only a legend.

But the major difference between Rivendell and Lothlórien is in feeling or atmosphere: "In Rivendell there was memory of ancient things; in Lórien the ancient things still lived on. . . ." (I, 453; *413*) Lothlórien is kept whole by the power of Galadriel, the Lady of the Galadrim or Tree-People, who rules alongside Celeborn. It is a land of golden flowers, *elanor,* and of golden-leaved mallorn trees; it is altogether lovely. The ancientness of Lothlórien may be suggested in a rather prosaic way: Galadriel is the mother-in-law of Elrond of Rivendell. He had married her and Celeborn's daughter Celebrían (who has since left Middle-earth), and they had three children, the twin sons Elrohir and Elladan, and Arwen Evenstar.

During the stay of the Company in her realm, Galadriel overcomes the traditional reluctance of the Elves to give advice to mortals by showing Frodo and Sam what may be seen in the Mirror of Galadriel.

The Mirror is not a guide to action, Galadriel tells the hobbits; they may learn much, but they must still make their own choices. Vision is no substitute for decision, and decision must come from intelligence and feeling.

Sam peers into the shallow basin of water, and then Frodo looks. He sees a figure like Gandalf walking along a dim road; he sees the Sea, and storm and battle, and then the Eye. This is the closest we ever come to seeing anything of Sauron, and it is probably symbolic or iconic. Wisely, Tolkien chooses not to represent him: any actual portrayal would have diminished the idea of Sauron, and of his evil. Here we see only the Eye, "a window into nothing." (I, 471; *430*) Since in traditional doctrine evil is only the absence of good, not a positive force in itself (as cold is only the absence of heat), total and consummate Evil must be total absence or negation, hence "a window into nothing." This negative quality does not mean that evil is without power: cold after all can destroy you quite effectively.

At this point Galadriel reveals that she is wearing, and wielding, one of the Three Rings of the Elves—Nenya, the Ring of Adamant. It is this Ring's power that is preserving Lothlórien and keeping Sauron both baffled and at bay. But we know that the Three Rings are somehow bound up with the One: its fate will seal theirs. If there can be a tragic aspect to an epic quest, the Elves—tall, noble, beautiful—are tragic figures. As Galadriel tells Frodo, if his mission to destroy the Ring fails, the Elves themselves will be destroyed; yet if the Ring is unmade, the Elves will lose power and will have to leave Middle-earth and forsake their majesty.

The next time we meet the Elves, in Book VI, they are in fact on their way out of Middle-earth. And yet, thanks to the gifts of Galadriel, especially her gift to Sam, they are not wholly forgotten. They leave a legacy of life and growth behind them. It is this bittersweet quality that so many readers find appealing about *The Lord of the Rings*.

Galadriel's gifts are enumerated (I, 485; *442*ff.) and we will be mentioning several of them in succeeding pages; besides her gifts to individuals, the Elves present to the party strong light boats, *lembas* or waybread, cloaks, and many other amenities, including rope, which Sam had forgotten to bring. The bestowal of these gifts is almost the last thing that happens as the party leaves Lothlórien to head down the great River Anduin.

The journey downstream is full of disquiet. Sam soon spots a log with eyes floating behind their boats. It is of course Gollum, whom the Council of Elrond had returned to our awareness; later events return him to the story itself. But, more immediately important, something is troubling Boromir; we are not told what it is, but he stares at Frodo almost avidly.

Tolkien said that people who complain that his story is too simple—all the good characters are just good, all the bad ones simply bad—overlook Boromir[3] (as they overlook Saruman, and Denethor, and even the Elves). Boromir is a mixture of base and noble qualities whose excellence in his chosen métier—war—redeems at least in part the wrong he's contemplating doing to Frodo. Very near the end of Book II is the fall (by seeking to wrest the Ring from Frodo) and redemption (by dying in defense of other members of the Company) of Boromir.

Fleeing Boromir, and wearing the Ring, Frodo attracts the attention of contending Voices, forces beyond his poor power to resist or even consciously to recognize. In the barest nick of time he escapes to continue his errand.

Five

A Short Interlude

LAWS OF THE WORLD

We may have compassed enough of *The Lord of the Rings* to be able to talk about the laws governing Middle-earth. One aspect of fantasy creation is the need for internal consistency: mere whimsy or arbitrariness is not allowable. Middle-earth is governed by internal laws that help us make sense of it. Most people who write about Tolkien agree on this; but each may formulate the laws a little differently. Here is one set:[1]

1. *The world of Middle-earth is providentially guided.* We have already seen a number of examples of a force operating beyond any power of the actors on the stage of Middle-earth: Bilbo was meant to find the Ring, and not by its maker (I, 88; *81*); it has been ordered that those seated at the Council of Elrond shall find counsel for the peril of the world (I, 318; *291*); another will seems to use Frodo's voice as he volunteers to carry the Ring (I, 354; *324*).

These shadowy powers are not identified in the text, but Tolkien tells us in Appendix A that the Valar, "the Guardians of the World" (III, 390; *351*), are watching over the fortunes of the denizens of Middle-earth. In the first two ages of Middle-earth the Valar interfered directly, with catastrophic geological results. Here in the Third Age, they manipulate to an extent, but they intervene mostly through agents such as the Istari, the wizards.

At the same time, and to a considerable extent, free will and choice are important. We have seen some cases in which choices seemed to exist and did not; more frequent are cases in which decisions can and must be made, and we see characters like Aragorn fretting over the consequences of the choices they make. *The Fellowship of the Ring* ends with Frodo having to make a choice (of where to take the Ring) and having exceeding difficulty in doing so. Only the intrusion of Boromir clears his mind; here it may be that Frodo knows the decision he must make but is reluctant to make it. And we will soon be looking at cases in which individuals must choose to ignore or violate some law or rule or edict in light of what they consider a higher duty and must suffer the consequences of their choices.

2. *Intentions create results, although the correlation can be unexpected.* A good action taken with a good intention produces a good result. And, paradoxical as it may seem, but in keeping with the notion of "felix culpa," an evil action taken with an evil intent will (ultimately) produce a good result. (Felix culpa, or fortunate sin, alludes to Adam's fall bringing Christ's redemptive presence into the world.) Bilbo's pity for Gollum saved Gollum's life long ago, and it may be important that Gollum be on the scene later. Similarly, Frodo's good intentions toward Gollum will save Gollum's life in Book IV; if, as Gandalf said, Gollum still has a part to play, that too may be important.

In the opposite vein, we have already seen how Saruman's intention toward Gandalf was evil; he evidently meant to keep Gandalf a prisoner at Orthanc; his deceitful method of luring Gandalf there was evil, and brought an (ultimately) good result: Gandalf was rescued. Many more examples of evil will marring evil will follow in the tale. The more interesting question may be, When will "ultimately" come to pass?

This indeed is one of the chief differences between Middle-earth and our world: we know that intention and result part company very often here—our actions often have a kind of result or magnitude of result very different from what we intended. We seem to have to say too often, "I never meant *that* to happen!" but in Middle-earth the attunement of intent to outcome is more finely calibrated.

3. *Magical and moral laws operate efficaciously.* That moral law really

works follows from what was just said. Good is ultimately rewarded; evil (through the production of undesired result) is ultimately punished.

Magic is valid in Middle-earth; it is part of its physical make-up. The chief practitioner is Gandalf, of course, who is not human, although he assumes human form. As a kind of archangel, Gandalf would be expected to have magical powers—and his powers lie, as noted above, largely in the realm of language.

Indeed, magic, as practiced by Gandalf, seems to consist of using language as a tool to gather and concentrate and focus the ambient energies of nature, so that with the words *"naur an edraith ammen"* he can thrust his staff into a bundle of sticks and set it afire. Thus what seems to be magic may be only (only!) a powerful sympathy with nature. When the travelers are about to leave Lothlórien, the Elves present them with handsome cloaks.

"'Are these magic cloaks?'" asks Pippin. The Elven leader replies only that they are cloaks which have the qualities of the places the Elves love—they have the color and the power of woods and waters, for the Elves put such virtues "'into all that we make.'" (I, 479; *437*) Again, the idea is that "magic" is a deep affinity with and understanding of the natural world.

Thus one might make a good case that although magic is indeed valid in Middle-earth, Tolkien gives us very little magic that is mere show or spectacle.

4. *States of mind can have physical power.* This, in a way, is a reciprocal of the preceding idea. If a mind can gather energies into itself and re-direct them, so the mind's own native energies can be projected outward to influence its surroundings. This is demonstrable by the effect the Nazgûl have on others just by being in the vicinity; everyone freezes in terror or blankness of mind. On the other side of the coin, this idea may help explain the "aura of leadership" shown by people like Aragorn or Faramir. When Aragorn challenges Éomer of Rohan to choose whether to aid or thwart him, he seems to grow in stature while Éomer shrinks. (II, 44; *42*) Proud Éomer is wonder-struck.

5. *The truth of proverbial wisdom is borne out in life.* The reverse of this is also true: proverbs are the distillation of experience, and there is plenty of proverbial language in Middle-earth (it becomes a question of language,

again). In keeping with rubric 2 above, in a world as finely tuned morally as Middle-earth, the same sorts of acts will have the same sorts of results over and over. Thus proverbs—"short cuts make long delays," "better late than never," "all that is gold does not glitter" (note that the last one is the reverse of our form)—are validated.

Some of the later books of *The Lord of the Rings* have governing proverbs or sayings, as we shall see.[2]

LAWS OF THE WORK

That was a partial formulation of the rules governing Middle-earth as a place to live, so to say; there are also rules governing the work that contains Middle-earth: literary rules, or literary techniques. Most of them are directed toward producing an effect of unity or wholeness: that Tolkien aimed for unification or at least consistency is shown by his remark about re-writing the book from the end to the beginning. (I, ix; *9*)

1. *Foreshadowing* is an obvious technique, of course, although it may be too early to develop the best examples. One may say that Frodo's experiences in the Barrow (underground, in darkness, beset by monstrous creatures, finding courage) are a foreshadowing of his experiences, similar but greatly enlarged in scale, in the Mines of Moria.

2. The use of *dreams* is a technique which is often a special case of foreshadowing, although dreams have a variety of functions in the story (see Chapter 16). There is an air of prophecy about some characters' dreams, while others seem to manipulate time in very different ways.

3. A third, which is a different statement of the notion of foreshadowing, is *parallelism* between the events of the two books which comprise a single Part (as Tolkien designated them) of the total fiction. You could look at the description of Aragorn when we first see him in the Inn at Bree (I, 214; *196*) and that of Boromir when we first see him at the Council of Elrond (I, 315; *289*); there are many similar elements in the two descriptions, meant to create *contrast:* the more functional when you consider that these two will represent the race of Men in the Company of Nine.

We can see many parallels between Books I and II, both in details and in large meanings (I follow Randel Helms closely here):

I recounts the adventures of a group of travelers—four hobbits.

II recounts the adventures of a group of travelers—nine walkers.

In each, the Ring-bearer and his companions proceed from a place of shelter, through perils to an elvish retreat (Hobbiton to Rivendell in I, Rivendell to Lothlórien in II).

In each, Frodo accepts the company of a Man associated with the kingdom of Gondor: in I, Aragorn, its king-to-be; in II, Boromir, son of its ruling Steward.

Each begins in festivity or cheer: Bilbo's party; the feast at Rivendell.

And each continues in its second chapter with lengthy scenes of imparting information: "The Shadow of the Past," "The Council of Elrond."

During each of these scenes the Ring is revealed, and in each Frodo must decide to deal with (bear) the Ring.

A sequence of adventures follows the decisions, ending with the Ring-bearer crossing a river (the Bruinen, the Anduin), and both river crossings test Frodo's will and courage.

Underground in the Barrow, threatened, the Ring-bearer puts courage and sword to use; underground in Moria, threatened, the Ring-bearer puts courage and sword to use (see remarks above).

On a hilltop (Weathertop), Frodo puts on the Ring and barely escapes detection in I; on a hilltop (Amon Hen) Frodo puts on the Ring and barely escapes detection in II.

Listing items in this way can make II seem a mere repetition of I, which all readers' experiences tell them it is not. There is great variety on the surface, in the tone, in the settings. The weight given to similar incidents is different: the river crossing at the end of I is an escape in which Frodo is nearly helpless as his companions fight the Black Riders; the river crossing in II is a conscious decision on Frodo's part to break the Fellowship and continue his journey alone if need be—the Anduin is Frodo's Rubicon to cross. Similarly, what happens in Moria is more significant than what happens on the Barrow-downs for reasons quite unrelated to Frodo's actions: in the former place Gandalf falls.

But the parallels do show, I think, that below the rich variety of surface incident and setting, Tolkien was continually linking things up and weaving the book tighter.

Six

THE TWO TOWERS: BOOK III

AN OVERVIEW

With Book III of *The Lord of the Rings,* the first half of *The Two Towers,* the War of the Rings can be said to have fairly begun. Three battles take place in it: the first is the attack of the Men of Rohan on the Orcs who have taken Merry and Pippin, a battle on which we have a curious double perspective, first seeing the smoke of the funeral pyre of the dead Orcs, then witnessing the attack from the ground-level, hobbits'-eye viewpoint of Merry and Pippin. The second battle is the attack by Saruman's forces upon Helm's Deep, which we witness. And the third is the attack on Saruman's stronghold of Isengard, which we hear about later. As readers, we are coming closer to the heart of combat.

We can think of Book III as having two major axes of action, revolving first around the hobbits Merry and Pippin and the Ent Treebeard or Fangorn; and second around Gandalf and King Théoden of Rohan, and the Men of Rohan, and of course Aragorn, Legolas, and Gimli.

Both involve an awakening:[1] the hobbits must awaken Treebeard and the other Ents from their slow, long-drawn, sleepy existence; Gandalf must awaken Théoden from the false sleep of old age and weakness into which his treacherous adviser Grima Wormtongue has put him.

Both these events are structured according to the laws of Middle-earth: providentially the hobbits arrive in Fangorn Forest, where, but for the self-ishness and mutual hatred among the Orcs and their leaders they would never have come; and by the law of providential control, Gandalf returns from his absence, enhanced and more powerful. The hobbits' arrival in the forest and the actions which follow from it are also a clear example of the reversal of evil intent.

Likewise, Book III may be said to exemplify the fulfillment of proverbial truth.[2] The "proverb" in question is that uttered by Éomer at Helm's Deep when Gimli rescues him from a band of Orcs in front of the gate: "'oft the unbidden guest proves the best company.'" (I, 177; *164*) I put the word "proverb" in quotation marks because this saying is in fact a Tolkien original and a counter-proverb at that: traditionally, the unbidden guest must bring his own stool, or is welcomest when gone, or knows not where to sit.[3]

At any rate, the saying is exemplified several times in Book III, as Randel Helms shows.

- Gandalf, unexpected and regarded with suspicion in Rohan after taking Shadowfax, returns to awaken the spirit of its king and save his kingdom.
- Gimli, unbidden, saves Rohan's next king.
- The Huorns appear at Helm's Deep unasked by its defenders and change the course of the battle (and their masters, the Ents, were certainly not bidden to come to Isengard).
- Finally, ironically, Grima Wormtongue, whose presence was by no means sought at Isengard, proves good company for the Free Peoples (though not for his host Saruman), by throwing down the *palantír* or Seeing Stone.

What are the effects of these victories for the Free Peoples? Seemingly positive but uncertain, one might say.

Many speak of the events in Book III as preliminary to later and bigger events in the War of the Rings, but of course that violates the logic of the narrative. Rohan and its warriors are awake, and free to act, and even heartened by the outcome of the set-to at Helm's Deep; what they may do later is unknown—especially in light of the isolationist mentality that has prevailed in Rohan until recently.

The appearance of the Huorns is much more hopeful: it suggests that there are forces deep in Fangorn Forest—deep within the realm of nature, speaking more broadly—that oppose the mechanistic evil spreading over Middle-earth.

And the *palantír* is quite literally a two-way device; it can help or harm depending on who uses it and how.

The use of guides in literary works involving a journey is both traditional and common-sensical, and Book III of *The Lord of the Rings* is no exception. Heretofore Frodo and others have been guided by strangers appearing rather suddenly on the scene—Tom Bombadil in the Old Forest, Aragorn at *The Prancing Pony*. Now familiar characters are used as guides to introduce us to unfamiliar ones. In Chapters 1 and 2 of Book III, Aragorn, Legolas, and Gimli set out to follow and rescue Merry and Pippin. In the course of that pursuit they and we meet the Riders of Rohan, the horsemen whose language and poetry exemplify Tolkien's knowledge of Anglo-Saxon language and poetry. Equally important, they meet the returned and changed Gandalf, now Gandalf the White.

But before that can happen, Tolkien himself has had to make some choices: with his characters separated, he has several narrative lines to follow. Frodo and Sam are across the river and can be dealt with later, but here we have two separate adventures taking place simultaneously, and Tolkien must handle both. There is (1) capture and flight, of Orcs and the two hobbits, and (2) tireless pursuit, by Aragorn, Gimli, and Legolas. Logically or chronologically one would expect them in that order, but Tolkien has reversed the order and created a time shift that both heightens suspense and lessens hope as Aragorn and the others meet the Men of Rohan and learn that the Orcs are dead and no signs of Hobbits have been seen. Only then do we revert to Merry and Pippin and find out what happened.

Under guidance we come to the central actions of Book III, which consist of preparation for, waging of, and the aftermath of the last two of the three battles mentioned above, Helm's Deep and Isengard; one we see with

Aragorn and the others; the other we are told of later by Merry and Pippin, when the group from Helm's Deep arrives at Isengard. An eventful nine days have elapsed between the breaking of the Fellowship at Parth Galen and the reunion of five of its members at Isengard, and Tolkien has carefully drawn his narrative lines together.

They are to be separated again almost at once as it becomes clear that a great struggle is still to take place—at Gondor, in Book V.

This then is an overview of Book III. The richness, as usual, is in the details.

THE MEN OF ROHAN

The blond horsemen called the Rohirrim, or the Men of Rohan, are represented as a proud, strange, intensely loyal people. They are certainly not primitive, but neither can they be called a people of refined culture. Like their real-life counterparts the Anglo-Saxons of early medieval England, their literary traditions are oral. Their language (Old English, for all intents and purposes) has a "strong music" in it. (II, 142; *132*)

The poem that appears in translation in the text at this point is not an example of Old English versification (it rhymes for one thing), but it is typical of Old English poetry in sounding the "ubi sunt" ("where are . . . ?") theme: Where are the snows of yesteryear? Where have all the flowers gone? Old English poetry is suffused with a sense of loss, a sense of human mortality and of the world's mutability, which is well represented here. (For a better example of Old English prosody see the poem in Part III, 92; *83*, which will be discussed in Chapter 16.)

The reference to "strong music" is not the first allusion to or discussion of language in Book III. Earlier we got our first sample of the language of Orcs. Two Orcs had been talking to each other in what Tolkien calls "their abominable tongue" and then one threatens Pippin with a knife, saying "'Curse the Isengarders! *Uglúk u bagronk sha push-dug Saruman-glob búbhosh skai.*'" (II,59; *56*) Most readers are glad that the sample of a truly ugly language is small.

Even this small sample suggests that the primacy of language in Tolkien's tale can hardly be exaggerated. It is a moral referent, as here (ugly language:

evil creatures); it is a device of characterization (the slow and thoughtfully descriptive language of Ents); a cultural norm (the varied but stern language of the warrior Rohirrim, or the speech of the Dwarves with its harsh integrity); and a field of play for Tolkien's imagination. No one who discusses Middle-earth can avoid talking about its languages, as Chapter 15 will show.

Linguistic spice apart, the Orcs' conversation (when read entire) tells us that there are three factions here: one from Isengard, that is, Saruman's troops; another apparently from Moria; and a third directly from Sauron's Barad-dûr, apparently called here Lugbúrz. The dissention and strife are apparently between the first and third of these, over what to do with the prisoners Merry and Pippin. It is a jurisdictional fight, if that term does not dignify it too much.

ORCS

This might be a good point at which to talk about Orcs, although there will be a fuller discussion in Chapter 14 below. These grotesque creatures of evil had appeared in *The Hobbit* and their appearance is as repulsive as their language is abominable: hairy, snaggle-toothed, apish, swart, slant-eyed, long-armed, crook-legged, etc. (there are several varieties). In *The Hobbit* they were frequently called goblins; that term is used here only once or twice: we are expected to take Orcs more seriously in this story.

Here in the War of the Rings, Orcs constitute the vast bulk of the armies of both Saruman and Sauron. They are the line troops, the ground-pounders, the infantry. That they are by nature both quarrelsome and treacherous bodes well for members of the Company, here and elsewhere.

ENTS

More pleasant to discuss are Treebeard and his fellow Ents, another "new" group (new only to us as readers, of course; they are among the oldest things in Middle-earth). It is a fact that some of Tolkien's most noteworthy scenes and motifs include trees: the Two Trees of Valinor in the First Age, for instance; their light, by a roundabout process, furnishes the light in the Phial of Galadriel, which she gave Frodo in Lothlórien. There is also the white tree, of similarly ancient descent, that grew and will grow again in the courts of the Kings of Gondor.

Likewise there is the Party Tree back in the Shire; there is the Old Forest and black-hearted Old Man Willow; there are the great holly trees which guard the Doors of Moria; and there are, loveliest of all, the golden-leaved mallorn trees of Lothlórien. And here we have a whole forest presided over by sentient tree-like beings.

For many years Ents have played almost no role in the political life of Middle-earth. They are, in fact, nearly forgotten, and have become the stuff of charming folk tales and stories for children.

Unfortunately, Ents seem to be among the creatures doomed in the passing of the Third Age, not least for the reason that their mates, the Entwives, have disappeared, no one knows quite where. The loss of the Ents will be unfortunate if only because they are wise and venerable. It is a matter of interpretation whether Treebeard or Tom Bombadil is the oldest being in Middle-earth: that distinction is claimed for both. (For more on Ents, see Chapter 12.)

As noted above, Book III is double-tracked. One line concerns Merry and Pippin, and their meeting with Treebeard, resulting (after due deliberation on the part of the Ent) in an Entmoot. The Entmoot is a gathering of Ents, and the term is borrowed in a manner of speaking from Rohan: the Anglo-Saxon "moot" or meeting was an assembly of people to discuss public policy and to make decisions on it. The moot is thought to be one of the first appearances of something like popular government in English history. The word refers to both the meeting and the place it is held; it survives in such ideas as the "moot" court, where hypothetical cases are discussed, and perhaps in so remote a descendant as the New England town meeting. The Ents, at all events, do discuss their situation and do decide to act, much to the discomfiture of Isengard.

MAN, ELF, DWARF

The other line, to which we should now turn, concerns Aragorn, Legolas, and Gimli, and their meeting with the Men of Rohan, and a little later with Gandalf. The two tracks will eventually meet in Tolkien's Chapter 9.

When Aragorn and his companions meet Éomer, he and his men are riding back from having slain the Orcs who had taken Merry and Pippin. The meeting is among other things a major culture shock for the Riders of Rohan when they learn that Aragorn and the others have just come from Lothlórien, the Golden Wood. They had hitherto supposed that this place of glamour was merely legendary, as many had supposed that Ents, and even Hobbits, were merely legendary. The sense of wonder among the Rohirrim is great, and as for legends Aragorn rightly observes that all may appear in them, because "'not we but those who come after will make the legends of our time.'" (II, 45; 43)

But even more important here than the distinction between story and reality—important as that may be—is the distinction between obedience and disobedience. Éomer is already in trouble on this foray for having exercised too much independent judgment, and now this trio of strangers is asking not only leave to roam about the countryside, but also the loan of horses to do it. He grants their requests.

This idea of disobedience as true obedience, or as obedience to a higher consideration than the letter of the law, has been seen before, in the actions of the Elf Haldir on the borders of Lórien in letting Gimli enter the Golden Wood. (I, 445; 406) It will be seen again in Book V where it saves the life of Faramir. It is a powerful nuance in a book whose business is so solidly with the establishment of rightful authority; it deepens the whole concept of duty, and underwrites the idea that individuals can and must make meaningful choices. Éomer is imprisoned for his choice, but his loyalty to his king is soon made clear and he is released.

THE RETURN OF GANDALF

A day after Aragorn, Legolas, and Gimli leave the Riders of Rohan, they encounter—against all odds—Gandalf. His reappearance calls for some comment. He clearly has been transformed from the Grey to the White; he has been in a sense elevated; he barely remembers that his name had been Gandalf. He says that "'I strayed out of thought and time'" and that "'[n]aked I was sent back.'" (II, 135; 125) That passive construction is a strong indicator of just how the powers beyond Middle-earth are aiding in its struggles.

Twice the Valar have intervened directly in the affairs of Middle-earth, with untoward results, but this time they have appointed agents or emissaries— Gandalf and his fellow wizards. Gandalf was sent originally as a guide, a counselor, an adviser. Now he has been returned and strengthened for the final and decisive clash.

Gandalf suffered death and "came back . . . with enhanced power" as Tolkien wrote an inquirer, and he added a very strong caution to anyone who might interpret Gandalf's return in a religious light: "though one may be in this reminded of the Gospels, it is not really the same thing at all. The Incarnation of God is an *infinitely* greater thing than anything I would dare to write."[4] Thus Tolkien warns against what is far too facile and superficial a kind of literary criticism: finding Christ figures. Gandalf is emphatically not one.

He is, however, for the time being the leader of the Free Peoples, and he explains to Aragorn, Gimli, and Legolas that the hope of the Free Peoples consists in keeping Sauron distracted. One means of doing so is the *palantír* or Seeing Stone, and to get that we must go to Isengard.

AT ISENGARD

Within the gates of once green and fertile Isengard itself, with its roads running like spokes of a wheel to its central tower, Orthanc, nature has been obliterated.

The organic has been replaced by the inorganic, the natural by the mechanical. Saruman has created an industrial wasteland (as we will see in Mordor, and as Sam saw to some degree in the Shire through Galadriel's Mirror): pollution, disorder, noise are the order of the day. It is pointless to ask what these turning wheels and thudding hammers may be fabricating at this industrial site; the very point may be that this is useless expenditure of energy, a mere mock-up of useful production. For Saruman has fooled himself into believing (or let Sauron fool him into believing) that he has emulated the great fortress of Barad-dûr, whereas in fact he has produced only a cheap copy.

Isengard has now been destroyed, and amid its ruins Gandalf and Théoden and the others find the hobbits Merry and Pippin lunching and smoking their pipes. Elrond feared the light-mindedness of these hobbits, and

Gandalf has more than once been exasperated by their seeming irresponsibility; but what the hobbits actually seem to have is an amazing ability to adapt to circumstances. Not many days before they were facing death at the hands of brutal Orcs, now they are availing themselves of good food (in true Hobbit fashion) and enjoying some of the Shire's finest tobacco. Among the material of war washed out of the depths of Isengard was Longbottom Leaf, and the presence of this luxury bothers Aragorn; he surmises that there is some hidden link between Saruman and the Shire. The accuracy of Aragorn's guess will be ascertained later; for now the tobacco matter not only suggests that very little is wasted in this tale, but will also have some bearing on the future of Saruman.

For Saruman is barricaded in his tower Orthanc, and comes out onto a balcony to parley with Gandalf and the others below. Once again it is a question of language; in this case Saruman's oratory and eloquence (which he himself has considered so powerful) are losing their effect. By trying to deal in different and contradictory modes of speech with different constituencies in the audience below him—addressing this one as an equal, patronizing that one, showing contempt for yet another—Saruman betrays the inadequacy of his rhetorical powers.

The duplicity of Saruman's speech reveals the doubleness of his mind—his treason against the Free Peoples in fact—so Gandalf casts him out of the order of the Istari, out of the White Council, and breaks his staff. At that moment a globe of dark crystal comes hurtling down from above; it is the *palantír*, thrown by Saruman's hireling Gríma in a gesture of spite.

With all his attempted charm and persuasiveness, Saruman seems startled by the sight of Hobbits among his hearers. This seems odd if he has been having dealings with the Shire about tobacco, but still we have been told that Saruman has long since fixed his abode at Isengard and never travels, so presumably he traded with the Shire through intermediaries, perhaps people like Bill Ferny or the "squint-eyed ill-favoured fellow" from the South (I, 213; *196*), whom the hobbits saw at Bree.

Later Gandalf explains some of this to Merry, but meanwhile Pippin is mysteriously drawn to the heavy crystal globe, which he had retrieved. *Palantír* means "that which looks far away," there are seven of them, and they are among the most ancient artifacts in Middle-earth. They could "speak" each to each, and the master stone, at Osgiliath, could speak to them all; few even remember that they existed, Gandalf tells Pippin.

We will hear more about the Seeing Stones in Book V, but the flood of information here is overwhelming Pippin because his burning curiosity has led him to look into the Stone, and he becomes the only person in the tale ever to speak with Sauron. The result seems at first disastrous; perhaps Pippin has given the whole show away, including, most importantly, his knowledge of where the Ring really is.

Pippin was, however, saved from revealing much at all, and if there is an element of the providential in that, there is likewise a clear reversal of evil intent in Grima Wormtongue's flinging down the Stone. It brought a good result from the point of view of the Alliance of Free Peoples. Similarly evil intent was reversed in Pippin's foolish act, for the net effect of his blunder is to confuse and mislead Sauron somewhat: he is thinking that the Stone has taken a hobbit, so to speak, rather than that a hobbit has taken the Stone.

Even so the party is just then attacked. Gandalf rides furiously toward Gondor with Pippin, and the others make haste to return to Rohan and muster its forces.

So ends Book III of *The Lord of the Rings*. With its double narrative line, it is a complex book, and yet it shows Tolkien's dexterous management of both narrative clarity and narrative momentum. It introduces two major groups of new actors, one of whom, the Ents, will play out their destiny largely within this book, and the other of whom, the Riders of Rohan, will have a large role still to play in Book V. It is more than just a smaller-scale preview of that book, for the events recounted here, particularly the recovery of the *palantír,* do much to determine both the shape and the result of Book V.

Seven

THE TWO TOWERS: BOOK IV

THE GARDEN OF GONDOR

East of the River Anduin, Frodo and Sam are beginning their seemingly hopeless task of reaching and entering the land of Mordor in order to destroy the Ring. Again as in Book III, familiar figures lead to unfamiliar ones; the figures and the stages of the journey at which they are met create a threefold structure for this particular book: first, Frodo and Sam encounter Gollum among the stony hills of the region called the Emyn Muil as they travel from the River to the Black Gate of Mordor. Then, finding that closed, they turn southward along the Ephel Duath, the mountains that guard Mordor's western face: in Ithilien they meet Faramir, younger son of the Steward of Gondor. And in the third phase, Gollum leads the hobbits in a generally easterly direction onto the Stairs of Cirith Ungol and into the lair of Shelob. Their encounters are with evil, then with good, then with evil again. Frodo asks himself even as they set out, "'will good or evil show [the way] to me?'" (II, 266; *248*) and in the event both do, whether through the opposite moral qualities of two individuals like Gollum and Faramir, or in the two sides of Gollum's divided nature.

Frodo and Sam meet Faramir and the other Rangers of Ithilien on March 7, and they are many miles south of the Shire. In a word, it is spring.

Many passages earlier in the tale show Tolkien's power to describe places both good and evil (Moria, Lothlórien), but his language here is particularly effective as he shows two opposite appearances of a season that should by definition be one of rebirth and renewal. Without quoting lengthy extracts here we can see the face of spring before the gates of Mordor—a repulsive landscape of slag-heaps and ash-pits and pools of filth (see II, 302; *282*). It is a region laid waste by Sauron's evil; it is sickening to look upon, as Frodo feels; even the light is "reluctant" to touch upon these surfaces. It is not simply that there is no life here, it is rather that life was here but it has been cursed, obliterated, wiped out. They said at the Council of Elrond that Sauron could ruin the land itself, and here is a small-scale example of his life-hating power.

By reassuring contrast Tolkien then shows us the garden land of Ithilien (once the garden of Gondor, we are told) where the hobbits and Gollum find themselves a few days later. Like so many other parts of Middle-earth, Ithilien is now uninhabited—but, even deserted, its vales and slopes show the loving care they once received. The passage beginning "So they passed . . ." (II, 326; *304*) conveys the picture Tolkien wants us to see: it moves toward increasing particularity, siting the landscape and the season's activity ever more precisely, enumerating with great zest a host of specific trees and shrubs and herbs and flowers—terebinth and thyme and anemones and asphodel—vegetation with mythic significance in some cases and listed somewhat in the cataloguing vein of elegiac poetry ("Lycidas," "Adonais") but to the very opposite effect, for life, not death, is celebrated here.

The floral life here teems, among pools and falls, and stone outcroppings. It is not just "here": it is a riot of growth; flowers are awakening, and they cover stones with blankets of color, and put out hosts of new blossoms. All this is conveyed in long rhythmic phrases (literally breath-taking to read) with special reference to the beholders (the landscape of Ithilien is an eye-opener for Sam, who is a gardener of long experience but little range) and it brings us, the readers, a sense of life abundant—exuberant and untamed, even—but gracious, and full of possibility, and of determination to thrive, even in the face of the evil to the east.

WHO IS GOLLUM?

Much of the earlier part of Frodo's journey in this book is taken up with developing the character of Gollum and his relations with Frodo and Sam. We and they first meet Gollum talking to himself: "'Ach, sss! Cautious, my precious! . . . We mussn't rissk our neck, musst we, precious? No, precious—*gollum!*" (II, 279; *260*) Gollum shows himself to be both hateful and miserable; he perhaps senses that the Ring is near, which would only increase his desire and his torment.

Frodo is seeing this creature, of whom he has heard much, for the first time. And like his cousin Bilbo long ago, he feels an unexpected emotion. We are allowed to see a kindlier side of Frodo's nature—instead of hatred for a contemptible evildoer, he feels pity for a pathetic victim.

Gollum is a classic case of split or dual personality, as conceived by the popular or literary imagination, not the clinical report. The idea of doubling, the doppelgänger, split or dissociated personality, fascinated the age Tolkien grew up in, and indeed the whole nineteenth century. James Hogg's *Confessions of a Justified Sinner,* Edgar Allan Poe's "William Wilson," the dissociated characters in Charles Dickens's *The Mystery of Edwin Drood* or his friend Wilkie Collins's *The Moonstone,* and most famously the hero/villain of a book published only a few years before Tolkien's birth, Robert Louis Stevenson's *Dr. Jekyll and Mr. Hyde,* are all familiar examples.

At any rate, the split may be described as between Sméagol and Gollum. Sméagol has pale eyes and speaks of himself as "I"; Gollum has green eyes and speaks of himself as "we." Gollum, in other words, is that side of the character pretty much totally identified with or consumed by the Ring. Sméagol has a tiny bit of personality that remains free of the Ring's influence. (Sam in his own mind thinks of the two sides, Sméagol and Gollum, as Slinker and Stinker, respectively.)

Gollum or Sméagol, however you care to think of him, was not completely eaten up probably because he was in fact a hobbit, or at least of Hobbit-kind, akin to the ancestors of the Stoors, as Gandalf told us long ago. (I, 84; *77*) As a hobbit, Sméagol was not especially ambitious for power; certainly he did not crave it or fantasize about what he might do with it (as Boromir, for instance, did). Besides that, Sméagol never actually wielded the Ring in any significant way; he just took it and hid under the mountains with it. In either aspect of personality, Gollum/Sméagol is deluded into believing that he once possessed the Ring; the Ring in fact possessed him.

Since Gollum is of Hobbit-kind, he and Frodo can understand one another. When Frodo confronts the sniveling creature, he is by far the moral and intellectual superior of the cur-like Gollum, yet he and Gollum "could reach one another's minds." (II, 285; *266*)

As might be expected, given the dual aspects of his nature, and given the proximity of the Ring (whose power seems to grow as it nears its place of origin or its maker), odd changes take place in Gollum as their journey proceeds. One occurs just after the confrontation mentioned above: another side of Gollum appears, saner perhaps, anxious to be helpful, in great fear of Frodo's anger, pathetically eager for Frodo's approval. We do not yet know what the manifestation of this "new" Gollum may bring forth, but like Sam we are entitled to be very suspicious.

This is the Gollum with whom Frodo and Sam must attempt to pass the Dead Marshes, for to travel on whatever roads might be in this region would be to deliver themselves into the hands of Sauron directly. The horror of the Marshes is more than their stench, or the danger of drowning; it is that, in the area called the Mere of Dead Faces, lights can be seen below the surface, and corpses are floating far below. Whether this is illusion, or magic, or some naturally preservative property of the water is not made clear.

Men and Elves and Orcs float there, the dead of the Battle of Dagorlad at the end of the Second Age of Middle-earth. Repulsive as the Mere seems, it does more than add to the general horror of the journey; it can be read as a token of hope, for in that battle Sauron was overthrown. It is in fact possible to see how often in *The Lord of the Rings* the truly horrid and the genuinely hopeful are but two faces of the same place or event: the Paths of the Dead that Aragorn and his companions must later ride are another example of this coexistence of contrary meanings, as were the Mines of Moria earlier.

But little hope seems possible now, as the three reach the end of the Marshes and have to endure an overflight of the Ringwraiths, now mounted on winged steeds of some sort (this is several days before Gandalf and the others see the Nazgûl on the other side of the River). Gollum is petrified with terror. After this, according to Sam's perceptions, Gollum seems in fact to be reverting to his earlier, more obnoxious behavior, and Sam is suspicious of *this* change also.

The split personality is nowhere more clearly shown than in the debate between "Sméagol" and "Gollum" (II, 303–5; *283–4*) which Sam overhears and in which reference is made not only to Him—Sauron—but also to Her, an allusion which mystifies Sam. When they come to the Morannon, the Black Gate at the northwest corner of Mordor, and find it of course closed, Sam wonders how sincere the ever-helpful Gollum is: he thinks "that the Sméagol and Gollum halves . . . had made a truce . . ." (II, 311; *290*), seeking to lay hands on the Ring at some later time.

Despite Gollum's incipient treachery, Frodo saves him a little later from certain death at the hands of Faramir's men, though to do so he has to trick Gollum into coming with him, an act that looks very much like Frodo's treachery, from Gollum's viewpoint. But Frodo does so because he has given his word to protect Gollum; he remembers that Gandalf had said Gollum still had something to do before the end; and Gollum is basically wretched and helpless—that is, he is pitiable, and pity colors Frodo's motives and actions.

So Gollum continues to accompany Frodo and Sam as they travel toward Mordor, despite Sam's very real misgivings. Somewhat later, an entirely different sort of change comes over Gollum; now he seems old, tired, weary of his existence. He has come back from one of his mysterious excursions and found Frodo and Sam asleep. Gollum looks at the two hobbits (who doubtless seem especially innocent and vulnerable because asleep) and an emotion strangely like affection, or at least the remembrance of affection, surfaces: gently he touches Frodo's knee: "could one of the sleepers have seen him, they would have thought [him] an old weary hobbit . . . [a] starved, pitiable thing." (II, 411; *382*) Gollum at this moment is an example of the evil effects of the Ring: he has lived a very long time, only to regret having done so; his life force or energy has not been increased or enhanced, only stretched or attenuated over countless years by the Ring.

Yet it seems as though for a moment Gollum has laid down the burden of the Ring, is no longer possessed by a lust for it or an envy of whoever has it—there is a sense of a *good* love in Gollum for Frodo. This does not last; it could not have; but it helps bring out our pity for Gollum. Up to now, Gollum has been found pitiable by nearly everyone—Bilbo, Gandalf, Frodo— except the reader. Now is our chance.

Sam breaks the moment, seeing Gollum "pawing" at Frodo; and Gollum's reaction is typical: just like anyone who has tried to right his own wrong action and been misunderstood in the act of correction, Gollum's viciousness is redoubled. We have to believe that Golllum's moment of emotional openness was a lapse, not a movement toward reform, because it comes just before the greatest treachery of all, as Tolkien suggests by the simile describing Gollum: "almost spider-like he looked now."

The Sméagol part, what there was of it, has pretty much disappeared by now; Gollum himself will vanish before much longer, and the two hobbits will find themselves entirely on their own as they come nearer and nearer to Mordor.

ANOTHER MAN OF WESTERNESSE

The hobbits' second encounter on their eastward journey toward Mordor is with Faramir, the brother of Boromir and son of Denethor, the Steward of Gondor. Faramir is, as his brother was not, a true son of Númenor. Faramir takes Frodo and Sam to a cave called the Window of the Sunset (or Window on the West), and the phrase, although it has literally to do with the orientation of the cave, could be applied to Faramir himself: he is a window on Númenor or the West as it survives, however attenuated, in the Third Age of Middle-earth; he is a window for Frodo on why the Quest has been worth undertaking—honor, nobility, and honesty are precious and need to be preserved.

Faramir as a character in the midst of the War of the Rings has many unusual qualities. For instance, he hates war even though he is a skilled warrior; as he tells Frodo, "'I love only that which [weapons of war] defend: the city of the Men of Númenor.'" (II, 355; *331*)

Equally unlikely, Faramir is a scholar, or at least he has had schooling in some of the ancient texts and languages preserved at Gondor; he was in fact taught by the person he calls the Grey Pilgrim, Gandalf himself. This scholarly bent may be a reason why Tolkien found Faramir a likeable character (see below). One of the small paradoxes of Middle-earth is that it is a realm in which education, considered as an institution or as a formal phase of life-training, hardly exists: in the Shire, for instance, cooking and gardening are skills thought more useful than being able to read, and hobbits like Frodo, who have a little knowledge of foreign tongues like Elvish, are looked at slightly askance. Yet it is also a place in which learning is highly valued, if only as the province of the elect. Faramir's desire to learn is admirable, but in the eyes of his father at least it is suspect.

One of the more fascinating psychological tangles in the story is the mix of attitudes Denethor has toward his two sons. As we will see more plainly in Book V, Denethor seems almost to hate Faramir, possibly in part because he and Faramir are more alike than he and Boromir.

Being more like his father, Faramir is less biddable, and more likely to exercise independent judgment without consulting his father or anyone else. In Ithilien, for instance, he tells Frodo and Sam that he is under orders to kill all interlopers in that region, and, he goes on, "'my life will justly be forfeit, if I now choose a course that proves ill. . . .'" (II, 350,; *326*) Nonetheless Faramir lets Frodo and Sam go, and gives them as much help as he can. He shows not only independence of judgment but also obedience to a higher law than the ordinances of Gondor.

At all events it is crucially important that Frodo and Sam meet Faramir: he must be able to report in Book V to his father and Gandalf that he saw them alive and still moving, so that Gandalf in turn can know that there is some purpose in continuing to distract Sauron's attention from Mordor, to keep Sauron watching Gondor and Minas Tirith. Some purpose still existing, Gandalf can plan his attack on the Morannon, the Black Gate of Mordor.

Faramir was a surprise to Tolkien. He wrote to his son Christopher in May 1944 about this entirely new character in the story: "(I am sure I did not invent him . . . but there he came walking into the woods of Ithilien)"[1] Tolkien's story-telling instinct may have known better than his conscious mind. What Faramir provides, besides a fascinating allusion to Robin Hood, with his woodland men all in green, is a balance: in myth and folk-lore stories of two brothers, one his father's favorite, are not rare. Often one of them fails a test and is punished; the other passes the test and is rewarded. Here the Ring is the test, and we have seen how Boromir succumbed to its allure. Faramir passes the test; he refuses to have anything to do with the Ring. The system of reward and punishment is a little more complex: Boromir redeemed himself by dying for his comrades; he was given the ship-borne funeral service due a hero, and Faramir saw the boat bearing him wreathed in light.[2] By contrast, if Faramir is to be rewarded, that will happen in due time.

The encounter with Faramir also repeats a familiar pattern of respite, rest, comfort, and counsel after dangers and miseries. The Dead Marshes and the Mere of Dead Faces would have been horror enough, but the land in front of the Black Gate is more horrid still. At that point, we were told that Sam fell into despair, now that "they were come to the bitter end." (II, 310; *289*) But Gandalf reminded us long ago that despair is only for those who see the end beyond all doubt, and the appearance of Faramir and his men validates Gandalf's wisdom. The bitter end is not yet.

But the stay with Faramir *is* only a respite; Frodo and Sam must go on, and when Faramir learns that their goal is the pass of Cirith Ungol and that Gollum is to be their guide, he is horror-struck and urges them not to go there, with that creature. But as is often the case, Frodo has no choices left, or at least he has no better option than to proceed eastward and upward by way of the Stairs of Cirith Ungol, and into the lair of Shelob.

SHELOB

Considerable background information is needed to appreciate Shelob fully. She is a child of the First Age of Middle-earth, having originally lived in lands now beneath the sea. She is the "last child of Ungoliant to trouble the unhappy world." (II, 423; *393*) Ungoliant was a great spider-creature of the

First Age; at the bidding of Melkor or Morgoth she destroyed the Two Trees in Valinor, the light from which passed into the jewels of the Silmaril, thence into Eärendil's Star, thence into the Phial of Galadriel, which is why that light is particularly hurtful to Shelob, the "child" of Ungoliant.

She may be said to be apolitical but not apathetic. She does not seek power, but only a monopoly on life: consumption of the free life of others, and for herself "a glut of life. . . . Far and wide her lesser broods, bastards of the miserable mates, her own offspring, that she slew, spread from glen to glen." (II, 423; *393*). Here, just as the fall into evil and ego of Morgoth in the First Age reminds us of Milton's Satan, the situation of evil guardianship and bestial incest reminds us of the picture of Sin and Death at the gates of Hell in Book II of Milton's *Paradise Lost*.

As to Shelob's relationship with Sauron, it is one of mutual self-interest. She guards this particular entrance to his land for her own greedy purposes, and he rewards her by sending her one of his victims as a tidbit from time to time.

Frodo and Sam come upon the great Shelob in her lair, and they fight her. Shelob has stung Frodo and is bending over him, at which point Sam truly unnerves her: this is a direct and literal confrontation between light/good and dark/evil; besides holding up the Phial of Galadriel and brandishing his sword, Sam cries out in Elvish, a sound that hurts Shelob simply by being Elvish. The language hurts her; and the light is an "intolerable light," "a dreadful infection of light," from Shelob's point of view. (II, 430; *400*)

Thus bested, Shelob slinks away to lick her wounds, but Frodo is taken by the Orcs of the Tower while still paralyzed by her sting. Almost the last thing that Sam learns is that Frodo is paralyzed, not dead: Shelob is no carrion-eater.

As parallels exist between Books I and II in *The Fellowship of the Ring,* so here parallels exist between Books III and IV in *The Two Towers:*[3]

- in each book a pair of hobbits must overcome geographical obstacles (the distance to Fangorn Forest—Merry and Pippin perform their feat involuntarily, of course; the passage of the Dead Marshes—which Sam and Frodo traverse of necessity but reluctantly);

- in each they succeed because of the reversed effects of evil intent: Saruman's Orcs get Merry and Pippin to Fangorn in III, Gollum (hoping to get the Ring eventually) guides Frodo and Sam through the Marshes in IV;
- later, each pair of hobbits encounters a figure of authority in a strange forested area (Treebeard, Faramir);
- in each case the figure was drawn there by a traditional woodland signal, smoke (the burning of the dead Orcs, the fire of Sam's cooking coneys, which he had let catch on green ferns);
- in each case the figure must decide what to do with the hobbits, and in each, after some questioning, the hobbits go with the figure to a shelter or cave where they are fed and sleep comfortably in the usual pattern of respite.

There is another parallel (and contrast) which underlies this last one, and which may be worth developing a little. Central to both Book III and Book IV are "forest" scenes, and Tolkien certainly allows us, whether intended or not, to compare the two, since we are introduced to each by a pair of hobbits who, like us, are entering the woods for the first time. The major contrast is in the relation of each woodland to human beings, Men.

Fangorn, Treebeard's forest, is nearly a virgin wood. Certainly there has been little human activity there: Treebeard's list of the four free peoples has Man last, and he speaks of Orcs, and wizards, and Elves, but says little of Men, although he can compare Ents with Men in their changeability, and Ents with Elves in their selflessness, putting his own race in a middle position (see II, 89; *84*).

Given the scale of Fangorn Forest (however long the 70,000 entstrides it takes to reach Treebeard's shelter may be), the hobbits find it formidable, and are properly awed. To hobbits (as a sub-branch of the race of Men) Fangorn is an alien, although not an unfriendly, place. In their conversations with Treebeard in his cave, the hobbits learn a great deal about his ancient and peculiar race.

To all this, Ithilien presents a series of subtle, not stark, contrasts. When they first enter the land, Frodo and Sam bathe in a little lake formed by a stone basin with a carved rim. Faramir's cave, which lies behind the water-fall called the Window of the Sunset or Henneth Annûn, was made habit-able by the engineering work of Men long ago. The trees mentioned in the passage I referred to earlier were planted, as were the garden flowers and shrubs, we may assume. The hand of Man (human beings, us) has very clearly been at work here. And to hobbits like Frodo and Sam (as a sub-branch of the race of Men), Ithilien and the cave seem a comfortable, home-like, and restful place. And in their conversations with Faramir in his cave, the hobbits learn a great deal about the Men of Gondor, descendants of the Men of Númenor.

Ithilien thus serves a double purpose as a contrast: first, as an example of a woodland country shaped by Men, and thereby enhanced in both beauty and utility to Men, contrasted with the untouched primeval quality of Tree-beard's woods, whose only outside contacts have been with Orcs bearing axes, and which are sprinkled with rather sullen tree-ish Ents. Tolkien is not asking us to state a preference here, because Ithilien also serves as a contrast to scenes of death and desolation through which Frodo and Sam have passed. Both Ithilien and Fangorn stand in affirmation of life, and in their difference, in affirmation of life's variety and richness.

The kinds of parallels I have been mentioning here, of discrete incidents and items or of large motifs, pretty much end at this point. What we have instead in the next two books is a careful paralleling and convergence of lines of actions controlled by time markers, as Gandalf and the others contend with the armies of Sauron west of the River, and as Frodo and Sam move closer to Sauron's headquarters east of it.

Eight

THE RETURN OF THE KING: BOOK V

In this book we return to the end of Book III, and return west of the River Anduin. Everything there has been drawing together to provide the action of Book V, which is the great war of Gondor, of which we see the greatest action, the Battle of the Pelennor Fields outside the walls of Gondor's capital, Minas Tirith.

The movement of the story up to the point of the battle is convergence: the troops of Gondor itself come into the city from various outlying districts, as Pippin and the boy Bergil witness. (III, 48–50; *45–47*) Likewise, the Muster of Rohan proceeds, and the Rohirrim ride as swiftly as they may south and east from Rohan to Gondor. Last of all, coming up the river from the south in a fleet with black sails are Aragorn and his companions, having traversed the Paths of the Dead. We go with Merry on the journey of the Riders of the Mark; we hear about the latter part of the passage of the Paths of the Dead after the fact.

PARALLEL JOURNEYS

The rather complicated itineraries of Aragorn and his companions and of Merry with the Riders of Rohan may be worth a glance at this point, as we pick them up from the end of Book III.

As we have seen, literary discussions allow us to speak of parallelism and convergence at the same time. Here Tolkien's art, and narrative necessity, lead us to talk about parallel journeys with a converging goal: different elements of the forces of the Free Peoples must go from Isengard to Rohan (where reinforcements are obtained) and thence to Gondor. Each element must travel according to the necessities of its duty: Aragorn must move swiftly to avert the crisis shown him in the *palantír;* Théoden must travel slowly to give his forces time to muster. Each traverses nearly the same ground, but Tolkien's narration shows how different it appears to each, and how many different historical facets the same terrain can display.

When Aragorn and his men, constituting the Grey Company, pass up into the hold of Dunharrow to begin their journey, we learn only that they hasten along the road between "lines of ancient stone" (II, 69; *63*) and that by sheer force of will Aragorn can bid his followers go on into the darkness. When Théoden and his men, including Merry, later come to the same place, they are a slow-moving army of thousands, and Merry has time to stare in wonder at the stones carved as the Púkel-men. They are images of a forgotten race, but somehow they resemble the Woses or Wild Men of the Stonewain Valley, or so Merry later thinks.

Aragorn's journey to Dunharrow is thus dramatic; Merry's is explanatory.

At all events, Aragorn brings his people, followed by the Dead, out into the Morthrond or Blackroot Vale, thence to the Hill of Erech, atop which is the Stone of Erech, thence southeast toward the Sea.

After the Muster of Rohan in Harrowdale, Théoden proceeds back to Edoras, where he intends to leave Merry behind. But Merry finds the means to ride to war, and the Men of Rohan proceed along the great West Road, urged to still greater haste, if possible, by Hirgon, a messenger from Gondor. They reach East Anorien, but there, enemy forces have blocked the road.

Since we have considered—so far, only in part—the routes by which forces move toward the war, it is also worth considering the perspective from which we see the war, and the importance of those whose perspective it is— the two hobbits Merry and Pippin.

We do *not* see the action "through their eyes" in any literal sense: Tolkien is still the third-person chronicler, but his eye is on them. We center on them and pay as much attention to the foolish Meriadoc and Peregrin as to Denethor, Gandalf, or any of the other great ones. They are fulfilling the prophecy of Elrond at the Council; he did not mean just Frodo when he said that "This is the hour of the Shire-folk. . . ." (I; 354; *324*)[1]

HOBBIT AS CATALYST

The opening of the war at this particular moment can be traced to a hobbit's actions—when Pippin looked into the Seeing Stone and was revealed to Sauron. Immediately, the Dark Lord ordered a Nazgûl overflight and prepared his campaign. Pippin's imprudent curiosity is bringing on all the action of Book V, or, more exactly, is affecting the timing of Sauron's moves; whether he moves in fear, or in ungrounded anticipation of triumph, he is putting out his pieces sooner than he meant to. Like the battle at Isengard, this Gondorean phase of the war is precipitated by a hobbit.

Besides the convergence of forces mentioned above, there are two parallel plot lines in Book V: one is Merry's swearing fealty to Théoden, and the actions of the Men of Rohan; the other is Pippin's swearing fealty to Denethor, and the actions of the Men of Gondor. In each case, that sworn loyalty saves the life of the ruler's child: Merry saves Éowyn's life at the Battle of the Pelennor Fields; Pippin causes Faramir's life to be saved in the Houses of the Dead.[2]

Both of these acts of pledging loyalty come out of the hobbits' instinctive sense of what is right. Both demonstrate their determination to do right. Indeed, if certain words expressing important concepts have resonated in earlier books of *The Lord of the Rings*, such a word dominates here in Book V, and that word is "will."

If there is a governing maxim embodying that concept it may be the one spoken by Éowyn as Rohan goes to war; in our world it is expressed as "where there is a will there is a way" (see II, 93; *84*). Éowyn is speaking to Merry about his ardent desire both to serve his royal master as he has sworn, and to go to war. She shows him the way, and indeed the very existence of the young warrior "Dernhelm" whom Merry accompanies suggests how ways can be taken when will is strong enough.

And Aragorn's will, too, is paramount throughout the earlier chapters of Book V. He has mastered the Seeing Stone and turned it to his will, and his second act of will is to take the Paths of the Dead, and to take with him the Grey Company through sheer force of will.

Who are the Dead of whom we are hearing so much? They are natives of these mountainous regions who had sworn to fight against Sauron in the Second Age, and then had broken their oaths. Isildur then cursed the oath-breakers, telling them """ . . . to rest never until your oath is fulfilled. For . . . you shall be summoned once more ere the end."""" (III, 64–5; 59)

To learn how Aragorn uses these Dead we must wait to hear about the last part of his ride to the coast. Just as Merry and Pippin told Legolas and Gimli of their adventures with the Ents and the storming of Isengard back in Book III, so here Legolas and Gimli tell Merry and Pippin of their ride with Aragorn and how Aragorn's will power commanded the Dead. And Gimli relates how they came upon the pirate fleet at Umbar and first para-lyzed it with fear and then scattered it in witless terror so that the hostile forces were completely routed.

THE TWO STEWARDS

Everything may be drawing toward the Battle of the Pelennor Fields, but there is much else to consider in the earliest pages of Book V. There is, for instance, the matter of Denethor's role or rule as Steward of Gondor, a stewardship which for many generations has ruled Gondor in the absence of the king. Denethor's exchange with Gandalf suggests how visions of duty can vary.

Denethor harshly tells the wizard how he will not be used in the plots of others, for his only duty is to rule Gondor, and that rule is his alone. Plainly Denethor's pride in his Stewardship—his de facto rule—is immense. But Gandalf replies from an even higher post of duty, a duty or charge not to rule, but to save, not a kingdom, but a world. "'For I also am a steward. Did you not know?'" (III, 33–4; 32)

Here Gandalf comes as close as anywhere to explaining his role in Middle-earth. He "was sent back," as he said some days ago, to care for, to foster and preserve, whatever can be brought through the storm of Mordor. His responsibility is greater, as his allegiance is higher. The royal beings for whom Gandalf is steward are collectively the Valar, under the authority of Eru, the One.

In the event, Denethor turns out to be mad, driven mad by his pride and by his grief over what seem to be the deaths of his two sons. His madness brings him to despair, but, as Gandalf had also said some time ago, "despair is only for those who see the end beyond all doubt." And Denethor thinks he does see the end that clearly, for he has been misled by the partial revelations of the Seeing Stone that he possesses. Denethor proclaims defeat for the West even as he lies on his funeral pyre, a defeat that seems to be signaled by, among other things, a fleet with black sails coming up the Anduin. Tolkien's irony is heavy here: we already know that it is Aragorn's fleet, bearing proudly the standard of the White Tree wrought by Arwen Evenstar and sent by Galadriel.[3]

Once more, at the moment of Denethor's self-immolation, disobedience has proved to be true obedience. Beregond the guard is disobeying Denethor's orders by preventing other guards from entering to kill the Steward and his son Faramir. (III, 155–6; *140–1*) "'[Y]ou must choose between orders and the life of Faramir,'" Pippin had told him earlier. (III, 123; *111*) After Denethor dies and Faramir is rescued, Gandalf tells the other guards, "'You have been caught in a net of warring duties. . . .'" (III, 159; *143*) Only Beregond dared defy Denethor's commands and save the young man.

In the Battle of the Pelennor Fields itself the Free Peoples suffer the loss of Théoden, King of Rohan, and they gain by the arrival of Aragorn with his warriors. Other than these, the most significant action on that destined field is perhaps the fate of the Captain of the Nazgûl. His steed is described as something like a pterodactyl, but less majestic than repulsive and odorous.

Confronted by the warrior Dernhelm, the Captain of the Ringwraiths cries, "'Hinder me? Thou fool. No living man may hinder me.'" (III, 141; *127*) His remark contains a world of dramatic irony. It is proverbial in its own way, having been formulated over a thousand years earlier by the Elf Glorfindel, the same Glorfindel who met Frodo on the road to Rivendell. Speaking of the Ringwraith as he was then, the Witch-King of Angmar, Glorfindel bids the others not to interfere as the King flees the battlefield: "'Far off yet is his doom, and not by the hand of man will he fall.'" (III, 412; *373*)

And like many prophecies, Glorfindel's is right, but not in the way the Witch-King/Nazgûl supposes: he is not protected from extinction; he is slain not by the hand of man but by the hand of woman and hobbit. The situation is reminiscent of *Macbeth,* where the witches promise him that "none of woman born/ Shall harm Macbeth"; but his nemesis, Macduff, was, it turns out "from his mother's womb/ Untimely ripped."[4]

Dernhelm then is the exception who takes away the Ringwraith's assurance of immortality; she slays the beast he rides; she and Merry between them strike at the Captain himself. And so too the ancient weapon that Merry received from Tom Bombadil months earlier on the Barrow-downs proves crucial: it goes up in smoke, but "No other blade. . . ," says Tolkien, "would have dealt that foe a wound so bitter . . . breaking the spell that knit his unseen sinews to his will." (III, 146; *131*)

Thus two earlier themes are reiterated and joined in this death scene: the idea that little or nothing in this book is wasted, and the idea that the struggle against evil is unending, for when the Captain of the Nazgûl perishes, he goes with a cry, a shrill and empty cry rising on the air that "was never heard again *in that age of the world.*" (III, 143; *129;* emphasis added)

BATTLE'S END

The aftermath of the Battle of the Pelennor Fields is caring for the sick and wounded. It is noticed that Éowyn, the erstwhile Dernhelm, is not dead on the field as supposed, and she is taken to the Houses of Healing. So is Faramir, who suffered a nearly fatal wound and a touch of the Nazgûls' Black Breath as he and his men retreated toward Minas Tirith, and who nearly died at the hands of his deranged father. So too is Merry, whom Pippin finds wandering in a deathly daze after the battle.

Scenes at the Houses of Healing are occasions for tests of folk beliefs, beliefs that Tolkien has said over and over contain more truth than they are given credit for, and that sometimes contain more truth than the acquirements of the learned (in a world such as Middle-earth, where learning is not, as noted before, prized highly, there can still be pretension to learning). The first test is the adage spoken by old Ioreth the nurse: "'*The hands of the king are the hands of a healer.* And so the rightful king could ever be known.'" (III, 166; *150*) That Aragorn can heal the three sufferers is a validation of the folk belief itself, as well as an added validation of his right to the throne of Gondor. The second test is the healing herb itself, the *athelas,* whose virtue Aragorn knows, even though Ioreth and the herb master—the chief pharmacist, as it were—do not. The herb master knows the name of the herb in several arcane languages, but does not know its real properties; his learning is to that extent false or trivial.

The episode embodies an interesting conflict between forms of knowledge. Tolkien himself was a scholar of course, of the highest order; no one valued book-learning more than he. But here he makes us see that book-learning should not look down on or scoff at folk-learning, folk wisdom, or traditions not kept in books. And the *athelas* works, as we knew it would; it is the same herb Aragorn used to treat Frodo's wound at Weathertop many weeks before.

(Somewhat analogously, the unlearned refuse to be patronized: when Éomer of the Rohirrim promises trinkets of various kinds to the Woses or Wild Men if they will show a secret path around the blocked road, their chief, Ghân-buri-Ghân, who can recognize condescension when he hears it, says that they want freedom, not baubles.)

As the process of healing goes on, Book V approaches its end with "The Last Debate," the council that parallels the Council of Elrond in Book II— not the same in scope, or in the imparting of information—but the same in purpose: namely to answer the question, What do we do now? To many readers, Gandalf is nowhere better than here. He tells those assembled outside the city that prudence would demand that we sit tight, build up what strength we can, and delay the inevitable end.

And one can almost see everyone nodding sagely, and saying that such a course would be wise, and Denethor would approve, and a prudent defensive posture would be best. But Gandalf then says, "'I said this would be prudent. I do not counsel prudence.'" (III, 189; *171*)

In effect, he goes on (and he has argued thus before): we cannot win by military means. Our only hope is that the Ring will be destroyed before we are. Aragorn's showing himself in, and mastering, the *palantír* was a very intelligent thing to do. Because of it, Sauron knows or thinks he knows, that if we, the Free Peoples, have the Ring we can use it. But still he is not sure; he is doubtfully watching: "'We cannot achieve victory by arms,' Gandalf continues, 'but by arms we can give the Ring-bearer his only chance, frail though it be.'" (III, 191; *172*) So if we do something rash, like mount an attack, he will think we are acting out of the pride of a Ringlord. That is what we want him to think, therefore we must attack.

So they set out, a puny army of perhaps 6,000 men, marching past once-great but little-mentioned Osgiliath, north through Ithilien, to the Morannon, the Black Gate; in effect they are re-tracing part of Frodo's journey, only in the opposite direction.

"The Black Gate Opens," as the chapter title says, and out comes the Mouth of Sauron, a spokesman who is or was a Black Númenorean, a mere human being, and nameless. Here is another piece of evidence that those in the service of Sauron lose their personal identity and are completely swallowed up in his ego, for his evil is to deny life, freedom, identity, to others.

At all events, the Mouth shows Frodo's cloak, the mithril coat, and the sword. Everyone blanches; even Gandalf *seems* stricken. But no—he asks that they show the prisoner, which leaves the Mouth nonplussed for just an instant. Immediately Gandalf shows himself as Gandalf the White, steps forward, rejects Sauron's terms, and takes Frodo's gear. We might well ask here why Gandalf is *not* in fact overwhelmed by defeat? That one instant of hesitation was enough to tell him that they have no prisoner. Gandalf knows that if Sauron or his minions had Frodo in fact, they would have the Ring, and if they had the Ring, none of this would be going on.

Despite its surface appearance, this confrontation sounds a hopeful note: it is the last of four confrontations between Gandalf and the forces of evil, and each time, the evil is diminished and less potent:

First, the Balrog was a creature of the First Age, a creature of Morgoth himself, of whom Sauron was but a servant.

Second, Saruman is a corrupted and degenerate wizard, an Istari of the same order and level as Gandalf himself.

Third, the Captain of the Nazgûl at the Gate of Minas Tirith was once a human being, a king of old become a wraith.

Fourth, the Mouth of Sauron is a living man still, and a bit of a coward at that: fear overcomes his wrath and arrogance and he gallops back to safety.

NARRATIVE TECHNIQUE

Again there are parallels between this book and the next, Book VI, but not of the same kind as before. The fated confrontation at the Black Gate is taking place on March 25, but see for instance III, 212; *192,* where we are told it is March 14 west of the River. As Book VI opens we have gone back in time; a few pages later in Book VI we are at the fifteenth of March, and so on.

A pattern is established here like that of many complex narratives: events in one time sequence are moving to converge with events in another time sequence. So the end of Chapter 3 of Book VI converges in time with the end of Book V: we are back at March 25. Through and after Chapter 4 of Book VI, the diverse timelines (of Rohan deeds, of Gondor deeds, of Mordor deeds) re-unite in a final single sequence to the end of the tale.

Before leaving Book V, a word should be said about Tolkien's role as narrator. As was mentioned in the first chapter, he is posing as a historian, transcribing material from the Red Book of Westmarch, compiled by Frodo and Bilbo, with supplemental material by Merry (see "Note," I, 37–39; *35–37).* But that pose seems somewhat transparent.

It may well have been Frodo or some other hobbit who put in the pointers to the converging time sequences. But some things at least could not possibly have come from the Red Book, that is, from the hobbits. A simple example occurs as the hobbits begin their journey; they are still in the Shire, are asleep, and a fox comes by, thinking it very strange that three hobbits should be sleeping outdoors, and thinking some mystery lay at the bottom of it. We are told that "He was quite right, but he never found out any more about it." (I, 108; *100).* Clearly the sleeping hobbits could not have known the fox was there, therefore they could not have recorded the incident, much less have added the gratuitous comment that he never learned any more about it. The way the incident is related is more characteristic of the whimsy of *The Hobbit* than of this book, perhaps not surprisingly since it occurs here early on.

But much later, near the Stairs of Cirith Ungol, neither Frodo nor Sam, since both are asleep, can know what Gollum looks like—the old wretched hobbit, the castaway of centuries.

Both these incidents are plainly the work of an omniscient narrator. And to point that out is not to criticize tiny flaws in technique, rather it is to compliment Tolkien's narrative skills—seemingly he can at one and the same time convince us he is a historian transcribing Middle-earth material, and, as an omniscient narrator, add texture, depth, and richness to the story without our *feeling* that there is any discrepancy.

Nine

THE RETURN OF THE KING: BOOK VI

Book IV ended with Frodo, Sam, and the Ring in desperate straits. Here in Book VI, measurably the shortest of the six books, a great many things come to pass; the significance of most of them is self-evident and needs little explication. It is a book of endings, to be sure, but also of beginnings, as one age of Middle-earth closes and another opens.

Book VI is a book about love and sacrifice. In it, the long-deferred love of Aragorn for Arwen Evenstar reaches its fruition as they marry; that marriage in itself involves sacrifice, for Arwen's father, Elrond, must pass into the West and she remain in Middle-earth, mortal. The love between Faramir and Éowyn of Rohan develops in this book, and they will rule in a restored Ithilien for many years. The hobbits' love for their homeland is evident as they scour the Shire, and Frodo's sacrifice on behalf of Middle-earth means he cannot stay there contented.

First of all, though, it is Sam's love for Frodo, combined with the quarrelsome nature of the Orcs in the Tower of Cirith Ungol, that enables him to rescue Frodo. The rescue is made possible, that is to say, by the combined effects of Good (Sam's love) and Evil (Orkish nature).

FRODO'S BURDEN AND
THE DESTRUCTION OF THE RING

Sam and Frodo eventually escape from the Tower and Frodo resumes the burden of the Ring, which Sam had borne for a few hours. They escape into a nightmare of hopelessness. The landscape they must traverse is broken, rough, and lifeless; the distance they must cover seems impossible, and the countryside is in a perpetual dusk. And of course the burden of the Ring becomes greater and greater as they near Mount Doom or Orodruin, the place of its making.

These are pages that many find unbearable to read or re-read. Still, in spite of the hellish quality of the experience we read of, the logic of narrative holds. Frodo and Sam have no idea what Gandalf and the others are doing in the west, but they have in fact ten days to get from Cirith Ungol across Mordor to Mount Doom. Frodo escapes March 15, and Gandalf's puny army arrives at the Black Gate March 25.

But they cannot go direct, because the plain of Mordor is full of Orc encampments. Here Tolkien's device of a feint—Gandalf's forces confronting those of Sauron at the Black Gate—has a happy side-effect: Frodo and Sam are picked up by a band of north-moving Orcs and hustled along at a forced-march pace, a pace they could never have set for themselves. And why the forced-march pace? Because this band is hurrying into position to attack Gandalf. And because many bands and companies of Orcs are hurrying toward the Black Gate, there is great confusion where roads meet and cross; in that confusion, Frodo and Sam are eventually able to slip away undetected.

So Gandalf's feint has two results: (1) it keeps Sauron distracted, drawing his attention away from the interior of his own land—as Frodo and Sam crawl slowly up the mountain, they see the flaming Eye in Barad-dûr, but it "was not turned to them: it was gazing north" toward the Black Gate with a full measure of hateful purpose (III, 270; *244*); and (2) it actually accelerates Frodo and Sam's journey toward the Mountain of Fire.

But the Ring has Frodo more and more in its evil grip as he and Sam near the mountain; it burns in his mind to the exclusion of almost everything else. Given such power in the Ring, it should come as little surprise that at the very end, Frodo elects not to destroy it. At the Crack of Doom Frodo puts the Ring on and vanishes. Then Gollum plays the part that Gandalf had long ago said he would: as Isildur cut the Ring from the hand of Sauron at the end of the Second Age, so Gollum *bites* the Ring (and its accompanying finger) from Frodo's hand and falls into the abyss to end the Third.

And Sauron passes away: "'The realm of Sauron is ended!' said Gandalf. 'The Ring-bearer has fulfilled his Quest.'" (III, 279; *252*) Still full of evil and malice, Sauron is but a black shade or shadow, powerless now that the Ring has ceased to be. He is swept away.

But as Tolkien observed when a correspondent asked him about it, Frodo "failed." The Ring overpowered him so that *he* could not destroy it, but his choice and his bravery had created a set of circumstances in which the Ring *could* be destroyed by other means.[1]

Thus the Pity that Frodo has shown toward Gollum several times proves to be the crucial emotion in the story, so far as the success of the Quest is concerned. That is, Pity for the hapless Gollum, victim of the Ring and by that victimization its hateful defender, caused Frodo to show him Mercy— to spare his life or plead for his life (as before Faramir and his men) more than once. Pity the emotion engenders Mercy the quality in action, and so, as Tolkien wrote in the same letter, Frodo's "failure was redressed" and Mercy has been or will be shown both bearers of the Ring. Here we are reminded of the discussion of mercy in *The Merchant of Venice,* and even though I will argue in a later chapter that Tolkien avoids coloring his tale with mere doctrinaire religious thought, we can even hear a faint echo from a mountain in Galilee: "Judge not that ye be not judged."

CELEBRATION AND CONSEQUENCES

There follows a time of great rejoicing, and of praise for Frodo and Sam and their deed. It is a time when the results and the aftereffects of the destruction of the Ring can be realized, such as the crowning of Aragorn as king of Gondor, and his marriage to Arwen Evenstar. Some readers have thought this union not adequately prepared for. It is certainly not insisted on, since it is out of the main lines of the story's development (although much more is told of Aragorn and Arwen in Appendix A). It might be said that Aragorn's feelings are concealed in language. When the Company early on comes to Lothlórien, Frodo sees Aragorn at a moment when he is far away in memory and looks more like a comely young prince than a road-worn Ranger; he says to some absent being "'*Arwen vanimelda, namárië!*'" which translates as "Arwen, fair beloved, farewell!" "'Here my heart dwells ever,'" he tells Frodo a moment later. (I, 456; *416*)

To return: the praise that is heaped on Frodo and Sam on the Field of Cormallen (in North Ithilien) leads to a much-discussed question: Has the book an unsung hero, and if so, who? "Sam Gamgee" is an answer frequently offered, but he is very much sung, as here, and goes on to be Mayor of the Shire six times, and eventually, many years later (it is said), goes to the Grey Havens and passes over Sea, last of those who have borne the Ring (see III, 471–2; *431–3*). So the question remains, unanswered, but useful for lively discussion.[2]

By the way, to pass "over Sea" is not a euphemism for "to die." As Frodo's experience at the very end of the story suggests, the Elves do sail West and do come to an actual country. (III, 384; *347*) It is Elvenhome or Eldamar, ordinarily accessible only to Elves, but, as Tolkien told Naomi Mitchison, "certain 'mortals'" important in the society of Elves may pass over Sea to Elvenhome. So Frodo, thanks to Arwen (III, 312; *282*), may go, and Bilbo may go, and at last Sam may go. Also, by unique privilege conferred by his fealty to Galadriel and his friendship with Legolas, Gimli the Dwarf may go.[3] And Tolkien told another inquirer, "Frodo was sent or allowed to pass over Sea to heal him—if that could be done, *before he died.*"[4] That is, Frodo and the others may pass out of Middle-earth into a kind of earthly paradise, but they will remain mortal; at some later point, unlike the Elves, they will die.

As for the events that immediately follow the destruction of the Ring: I said at the beginning of the chapter that not many things needed explanation, and certainly the happiness and festivity that ensue in Gondor and throughout Middle-earth seem to come in course. Still, questions remain in the minds of some readers. In the thrill of victory in the War of the Rings, and in the sense of new beginnings, the matter of Aragorn's right to the throne of Gondor can easily be slighted. Here as in few other places in his story, Tolkien can show us that right by combining highly traditional elements and symbols with potent signs of growth and change.

In fact it is not even the throne of Gondor that is at issue: Aragorn becomes Elessar, monarch of a Reunited Kingdom consisting of Gondor in the south and the remnants of Arnor in the north. He becomes king of the lands in which the Shire lies, and he never forgets the great role the hobbits played in his being able to take the throne. Under the protection of Elessar (who also calls himself "Telcontar," or "Strider"), the Shire keeps its well-deserved autonomy.

But the question is still a good one: By what right or claim does Aragorn, this one-time Ranger of the North, known as Strider to some folks in those parts, and to other less friendly ones as Long Shanks, become the greatest monarch in Middle-earth? In the last moments of his life Denethor snarls that he will not in his old age become steward to one with an inferior claim to the throne of Gondor (see III, 156; *142*).

Even though anyone of the line of Isildur would have a valid claim to the throne, and even though Denethor is nearly mad at the moment he speaks, what he is saying needs to be answered. It is surely not just blood—not just being of a certain lineage—that qualifies Aragorn at this historical (and historic) juncture. If he is eligible to be king, why was not his great-grandfather?

The War of the Rings has twin objects: both the overthrow of arbitrary tyranny in the defeat of Sauron and the restoration of rightful authority in the accession of Aragorn. These two events happening together will ensure a long era of peace and prosperity for Middle-earth. In Aragorn we have a nicely traditional meeting of the man and the moment.

Even though Isildur was the elder son of Elendil (Anárion having been the younger), his is the lesser line, at least in Denethor's eyes. Isildur ruled Gondor briefly, but then departed to assume the throne of the northern kingdom, Arnor. On his journey north he was ambushed by Orcs: that was the moment at which the One Ring was lost for a very long time, until the hapless Déagol found it on the river bottom. Thus Isildur gave up one set of kingly responsibilities and never was able to assume the other.

Still, by primogeniture, which generally prevails in Middle-earth, Isildur's heirs have claims. But Aragorn has much more:

- he has military prowess; his strategic skill as well as his courage lead the forces of Good to victory; he is second only to Gandalf in this role;
- he has the ruling powers of the rightful king, as we have seen;
- more than just generalship, he has leadership: he inspires Men (and others) to obey willingly, or even unwillingly. His willpower alone brings his forces through the Paths of the Dead and puts those very Dead under his control;
- his willpower also matches and masters that of Sauron; he can take control of the Seeing Stone, the *palantír* of Orthanc, away from the Dark Lord. This act is not only a stratagem to keep Sauron's attention off Mordor (and thus give Frodo a better chance), but it is also a demonstration of Aragorn's very real powers. And the destruction of the Ring, which Aragorn's acts and character help make possible, clears the way for the very concept of a Reunited Kingdom that he can justly rule.

Aragorn has still other claims to the throne of Gondor and Arnor. He has the support of other great leaders in Middle-earth (as well as the endorsement of plain folk like Hobbits):

- Galadriel has long since given Aragorn her blessing. When the Company leaves Lothlórien, she gives him a beautiful silver brooch with a great green stone, telling him to take the name and title that are his by right: "'Elessar, the Elfstone. . . . '" (I, 486; *442*)
- Gandalf has done all his work in order to destroy Sauron of course but also to bring about the moment of Aragorn's rule. His work is over; his stewardship, of which he had reminded Denethor earlier, is nobly completed. Just as the task of destroying the Ring had to be fulfilled within Middle-earth, so the task of governing Middle-earth wisely afterward must be.
- Elrond at last adds his blessing. Arwen Evenstar is Aragorn's bride-to-be, and Elrond's daughter and Galadriel's granddaughter; once the throne is re-established, the marriage can take place. On Midsummer Eve a great procession arrives at Minas Tirith: Glorfindel, and Galadriel, and many more; and last of all, Elrond bearing the sceptre of

Annúminas (see III, 310; *279–80*), which he surrenders, and Aragorn and Arwen can be wed.

The sceptre is only one symbol of Aragorn's rightful rule. Annúminas was the chief city of the old kingdom of Arnor (as Elrond had mentioned long before at the Council [I, 320; *294*]), and the sceptre had come from Númenor itself, where it had been crafted more than five millenia before. Elrond has the sceptre by right and has the right to bestow it since his brother Elros was the first king of Númenor, and Elendil, and Isildur, and of course Aragorn himself are all descendants of Elros and are Elrond's nephews (with many hundreds of "great-"s prefixed).

THE WHITE TREE

There is another object that proves Aragorn's claim and which more than rivals the sceptre in ancientness, but it is a work of nature, not of Man. On the mad ride from Orthanc to Gondor, Pippin hears Gandalf singing to himself, and puzzles over the line about "*Seven stars and seven stones/ And one white tree.*" (II, 258; *239*) The seven stars turn out to be the constellation the hobbits call the Sickle, which they had seen long ago at Bree (see p. 14); the seven stones, Pippin soon learns, are the Seeing Stones, the *palantíri,* which he had gotten into so much trouble about; but the tree remains a riddle.

In Minas Tirith itself he notes that the surcoats of the livery worn by the Guards of the Citadel have a white tree embroidered on them, and a moment later in the Court of the Fountain of the Citadel he sees a dead tree that seems to have been left lying about in this otherwise scrupulously neat place; wondering why, he remembers Gandalf's softly sung words.

Pippin had not of course been at the Council of Elrond to hear the Elf explain how there grew in the courts of the king at Minas Tirith (as it is now called) "a white tree," scion of a tree from Númenor, itself scion of a tree from Elvenhome, itself scion of a tree from Valinor, the Uttermost West. The white tree thus represents a continuity even deeper in time than the sceptre—or it would if it were not dead.

But not until the War is over and Aragorn is crowned King Elessar is the matter of the white tree clarified (and then apparently not for Pippin himself). Gandalf takes Aragorn high up above the city and shows him a seedling of the white tree growing amid the snows. Gandalf recounts the same lineage for the tree as Elrond had given and says that this sapling is descended from the "'Eldest of Trees. . . . it has lain hidden on the mountain, even as the race of Elendil lay hidden in the wastes of the North.'" (III, 309; *279*) So the white tree is symbolic of the re-establishment of Aragorn and his line on the throne, and of the persistence (if nothing more) of Men.

Aragorn takes the sapling back to the Court of the Fountain and plants it in place of the dead tree Pippin saw. By June it is in full blossom, wearing white for his wedding and his reign.

Following the rejoicing and the re-establishment of rightful authority in the person of Aragorn, there come "Many Partings." This chapter is clearly meant to recall the "Many Meetings" of Book II, although, given all the intervening events, the scale, number, and finality of the partings is vastly greater.

The body of King Théoden is returned in state to Rohan to rest in the eighth mound on the east side of the Barrowfield, and Merry must say farewell to him. At Edoras, Elrond and Arwen are parted forever in perhaps the most poignant farewell in a poignant chapter. Then the remainder of the party rides on to Isengard, where they find that Treebeard has undertaken a great work of restoration, replacing stone and metal with trees, and grass, and orchards wherever possible. They also learn that he has soft-heartedly let Saruman and Gríma go (and a little later they actually meet the surly former wizard on the road).

At last they come to the point where Celeborn and Galadriel must turn east toward Lothlórien, and part from Elrond, Gandalf, and the hobbits, who are bound for Rivendell to see Bilbo. The elders of the Age linger, loath to separate, speaking only mind to mind as the hobbits sleep nearby. They remember all that they have done and suffered, and consider all that others must do in the age to come (see III, 325–6; *294*). These conversations, besides being a revelation of mental powers hitherto not shown to the world at large, are also incidents that no hobbit could have recorded.

Eventually they part until it is time for the Three Rings and their holders to leave Middle-earth. The "'power of the Three Rings . . . is ended,'" Gandalf tells Aragorn (III, 308; *278*), settling that matter for good and all. Galadriel's Nenya, Elrond's Vilya with its stone of blue, and Gandalf's red Narya, given him by Círdan the Shipwright, become another element of the "magic" leaving Middle-earth.

TAKING BACK THE SHIRE

When Frodo and his friends return to the Shire, after a visit with Bilbo at Rivendell, they find it in the hands of ruffians and corrupt officials, mostly Men, assisted by a few weak-willed hobbits. One of the evils of Shire government is simply that there is more of it—more rules, more petty bureaucrats. Also mills and factories have replaced trees and hedgerows, and there is a general air of both degradation and indifference.

What attitudes have led to the present condition of the Shire? One is reminded of Edmund Burke's aphorism: "The only thing necessary for the triumph of evil is for good men to do nothing."[5] There is the natural desire of even very good men like Farmer Cotton not to get involved. There is the desire of individuals like Lotho Sackville-Baggins for wealth and power, with no one to hinder him, and the over-reaching that comes in the name of that desire. Lotho has become merely a figurehead; the ruffians are really in charge, as Frodo tells Sam. (III, 352; *318*) The real power seems to be in the hands of a character named Sharkey, who has arrived on the scene relatively recently.

Evil and corruption in the Shire are expressed in ways we have seen before—in the destruction of living things like trees and in the process of industrialization, as in Mordor, and as at Isengard. Farmer Cotton tells the hobbits that the mills no longer grind corn (grain) but produce mostly fumes and vile odors; their waste water is polluting the pure streams of the Shire. Cotton is right in observing that Sharkey and his henchmen are making the Shire into a wasteland; it seems to be what they are good at (see III, 361; *326*).

Tolkien is showing us that it is rather naïve to suppose that the destruction of the Ring would do away with evil altogether. Nor are battles and deeds, however glorious, sufficient for the task. You can never take it easy; as Gandalf put it long ago, "'Always after a defeat and a respite, [evil] takes another shape and grows again.'" (I, 81; *76*) It is not difficult to see what shape Tolkien envisions evil taking as the Fourth Age gets underway. Evil is at any rate in people, in hearts and wills, not just in rings.

The passing of "Sharkey" (who is Saruman of course) suggests this: the Worm(tongue) at last turns and stabs his master; bowmen instantly destroy Gríma himself. The body which Saruman has inhabited is mortal, and his spirit rises from it like a gray smoke: "For a moment it wavered, looking to the West"—for forgiveness? restoration? repatriation?—but the pathetic entreaty is rejected, and the misty figure sighs—and is "dissolved into nothing." (III, 370; *334*) Even in his final gesture, it seems, Saruman can manage only a faint imitation of his master Sauron.

THE GREY HAVENS

So the Shire is scoured clean, at the cost of the lives of some hobbits and more Men, and we pass into a final chapter called "The Grey Havens," which is a kind of postscript, or acts as a coda to a piece of music. It resolves things and to an extent satisfies the mind.

The chapter really points in two directions: toward endings and toward beginnings. It is the end for the wearers of the Three Rings, and it is the place where the magnitude of Frodo's sacrifice becomes apparent. He is ill in March, on the anniversary of his poisoning by Shelob, and again in October, on the anniversary of his stabbing at Weathertop. Even more painful than the wounds inflicted by the Quest, although less obvious, is Frodo's missing the Ring; in dreary moments he longs for it. Finally he decides to accept the place Arwen offered him. Having sacrificed his health and his well-being, Frodo must now give up his home and his beloved people. And so he will pass over Sea to the Blessed Realm to heal him of his grievous wounds.

But even more emphatically, "The Grey Havens" is about fresh starts. New gardens, trees planted or re-planted throughout the Shire, a bumper crop of babies, all mark the wonderful year of 1420. In this year the vineyards flourish, the tobacco crop flourishes, and the barley is so fine that beer made from it is the standard for a long time to come: a really excellent tanker of it is known as "'proper fourteen-twenty.'" (III, 375; *339*)

The key to much of this fecundity and fertility is Galadriel's gift to Sam, soil from her orchard, as well as the acorn of a mallorn tree, which Sam plants to replace the old Party Tree under which the story began. The mallorn shoots up and makes the Shire beautiful and famous: it becomes one of the loveliest mallorn trees in all of Middle-earth.

So even though the Elves must pass into the West, they leave something of themselves in the Shire and in Middle-earth; they are not gone and forgotten. Nor are Frodo and his deeds: as he adjures Sam, "'You [must] keep alive . . . memory . . . , so that people will remember the Great Danger and so love their beloved land all the more.'" (III, 382; *345*)

Thus this final chapter embodies the paradoxical theme that runs throughout *The Lord of the Rings:* the inevitability of change and the need to restore what has been changed. Tolkien argues for the inevitability of large historical processes, which we must accept, but also for the restoration of former states of peace and plenty, of former grace and beauty, whose end or diminution we must not accept. Tolkien is a conservative, but for him the antonym of "conservative" is not "liberal" or "progressive"; it is "destructive."[6] So the passing of the Elves (irrecoverable change) and the Scouring of the Shire (restoration of what had been changed) are both necessary.

Thus, although much that had flourished in the Third Age will disappear, much that had fallen into disuse or disrepair will be returned: Aragorn on the throne of Gondor (or, even better, of the Reunited Kingdom) being only the obvious example. We have seen that Isengard is being returned to a natural state; under Faramir, Ithilien will once more become the garden of Gondor, and even the old king's head at the Crossroads there will again sit on its pedestal.

Frodo has told Sam to read from the Red Book of Westmarch to the younger generation to keep memory alive, and that suggests that one way continuity can be found is through art—specifically, story. We are in the same tale as Beren, Sam observes (II, 408; *379*), and "'What a tale we've been in,'" he adds after the story is pretty much over. (III, 281; *254*) Much earlier Frodo had rather deprecated the idea that the story of his adventures would be in any way memorable (see II, 408; *379*), but on the Field of Cormallen, after choruses of praise for the heroes, a minstrel of Gondor announces that he will sing a freshly made ballad about Frodo and the Ring.

So Frodo and Sam and their companions are part of a tale that has been in the process of unfolding since the First Age of Middle-earth. Having come to the end of this commentary on Tolkien's portion of the tale (accepting for the moment his pose as chronicler), I can only agree with his characterization of its greatest defect: "the book is too short." (I, x; *10*)

Part II

Introductory Note

These chapters place and describe the various inhabitants of Middle-earth. The descriptions are limited, in that they are meant *only* to help readers of *The Lord of the Rings*. Volumes and volumes of preliminary and antecedent material have been published, mostly under the editorship of J. R. R. Tolkien's son Christopher, and they show much of the process of the development of Middle-earth's universe.

To J. R. R. Tolkien, Middle-earth was a living entity. His ideas about it, the stories he crafted of its inhabitants, and their deeds of folly or wisdom were constantly evolving. Not only did *The Lord of the Rings* fix in print only a brief moment of an ages-long saga (although a very important moment!), it itself provoked further historical and archival material, as readers wrote in with questions and as Tolkien continued to prepare the antecedent material which was his true love, and which eventually appeared in part as *The Silmarillion*. Christopher Tolkien tells us that the final volume of *The History of Middle-earth* contains writings from the last year of his father's life (1972 or 1973).

Thus differing and even contradictory versions exist of a number of matters such as the identity of Glorfindel, the whereabouts (and names) of the other two of the five wizards or Istari sent to Middle-earth, and so on. Again, the "facts" I present here are only those most consistent with the narrative logic of *The Lord of the Rings* itself, a story that in turn presents only a small section through a complex imaginative structure.

Where possible, the material presented is designed simply to further the understanding of those reading the three volumes of the story. Thus a recounting of all the adventures of the Elves during the First and Second Ages is clearly out of place (although the stories are readily available), while some discussion of the ancient enmity between Elves and Dwarfs can help the reader understand why Gimli Glóin is so rudely treated at the borders of Lothlórien. Likewise, Galadriel's biography exists in several versions: her story has "severe inconsistencies," Christopher Tolkien tells us, and it "underwent continual refashioning."[1] But we need that version embedded in, or at least most consistent with, *The Lord of the Rings* to understand why her refusing the One Ring and saying "I pass the test" (I, 474; 432) is especially poignant.

I have not devoted a separate chapter to Hobbits because Tolkien himself covered them so thoroughly in his "Prologue." Still, the lore is so rich that a few observations on Hobbits along the way may, I hope, be forgiven.

The chapters attempt to answer several questions of origin, where the information is available:

1. When did Tolkien first think of Hobbits, or Ents, or whatever creatures are under discussion? Clearly, one cannot answer this question about entities like Men (human beings), and it is not much easier to assign a date to his first concerns with Elves—they were part and parcel of the very beginnings of Middle-earth.

2. Where does Tolkien place the origins of various groups in his history of Middle-earth? This question is interestingly different from the first: Ents, for example, came to Tolkien rather late in the process of composing *The Lord of the Rings,* yet he tells us that they are among the oldest of creatures living in Middle-earth. Here a certain amount of inconsistency was left to be dealt with, as Tolkien himself acknowledged, and the reconciliation never wholly came.

3. What is the status or stature of the various groups or races as the Third Age ends? What will become of them? Not every case is as clear as the Elves':

indeed, even among the Elves we cannot suppose that every one left at the same time as Elrond and Galadriel. Those two stood for the end, so to say, but the withdrawal must have been rather gradual—How big a fleet could Círdan have?

In any event, I have tried to bring out whatever hints may exist as to the futures of Middle-earth's peoples.

The chapter on Men required some sub-divisions, and it has become something of a catch-all. While it treats of Men in their relationship to Elves (Faramir and other descendants of the old Númenoreans), and talks of images of ancient men (Púkel-men), and their descendants the Woses, those entities that used to be Men, the Ringwraiths, are treated elsewhere—in the chapter on evil things. Here you will find a few words on Hobbits, whose relationships to Men Tolkien both emphasized in the "Prologue" and portrayed in the citizenry of Bree.

The chapter on languages required somewhat different organization from the others. No one can expect to equal Tolkien in his treatment of language in Middle-earth: language was the root and inspiration and guiding force of the whole enterprise, and Tolkien, in the Appendices and in such places as his essay on translation, has given us a wealth of information. All I have tried to do here, taking myself as a fair example of the non-specialist reader, is explain the families of languages, the salient characteristics of the languages mentioned, the esthetic qualities assigned to various tongues, the systems of characters (alphabets) used, and similar matters—so that *I* could understand them. I have also tried to find available translations (by Tolkien himself if possible) of the foreign language material, placing them either here or at the appropriate point in the commentary on the narrative itself. In all these activities, I beg the indulgence of cleverer or more linguistically gifted readers.

Ten

THE ELVES

Sadness and wisdom in the countenance of Faramir, a true son of Númenor, suggest the close ties between Men as Tolkien portrays them and the Elves, who were the first love and the first impetus of his storytelling. Middle-earth is inseparable from Elves; unlike Ents or even Hobbits, they were there from the beginning: Elves were in the poems of Tolkien's teenage imagination, and they were characters in the first story that he actually wrote down.[1]

Elves were the heroes and heroines of the saga at which he labored all his working life, and that saw publication only in 1977 as *The Silmarillion*. One of the poignant features of *The Lord of the Rings* is that in it we are seeing the Elves only at the end of the Third Age, as they prepare to leave Middle-earth for the last time, after their long tenure, and their great griefs and joys, in the world that they love. We see them in the fullness of their wisdom and sadness.

Elves were Men made wonderful. They were certainly not the spry creatures of children's stories, nor the little fellows who make Christmas toys, nor the elusive sprite of John Keats's "Ode to a Nightingale" ("deceiving elf"). "Elves" was not the best term for the creatures Tolkien visualized, for they needed to be distinguished from the wee quaint fairies and pixies of Continental tradition. As he wrote to Naomi Mitchison, "they really represent Men with greatly enhanced aesthetic and creative faculties, greater beauty and longer life, and nobility. . . ."[2]

Tolkien's letter to Mitchison is worth reading in full for the relation of Elves to Men, for Faramir (mentioned at the outset here) has a kinship to Elves, as does Aragorn, the king-to-be. Both are descendants of loyal Númenoreans, and the noble lines of Númenor arise from the kingship of Elros. Elros was the brother of Elrond, and they were children of an Elf-Human union, and, being so, had to choose irrevocably to be Human or Elven. Elros chose the former, and Elrond the latter. In Men like Faramir and Aragorn, Elven blood (genetic relationship) and Elven character (nobility) are preserved.

And Galadriel is stating exactly what happened to the concept of "Elf" in our Age when she tells Frodo that the Elves will diminish and "become a rustic folk of dell and cave. . . ." (I, 472; *431*) Tolkien's gift for reconstituting folklore is nowhere more apparent than here. He shows us, fictionally speaking, what those beings we think of as brownies or sprites really were in the age that was, and how much our ignorance has demeaned them.

The dividing line—the greatest of Elven differences from Men—was mortality vs. immortality. The test that the so-called loyal Númenoreans passed, long after Elros's day, was in not rebelling against the decrees of the Valar, and not seeking immortality. Immortality in the ordinary course of nature is a basic characteristic of being an Elf; immortality for Elves needs no comment—they simply have it. The *desire* for immortality is one of the hungers of Men; the story of the struggle to live forever properly belongs to the story of Men.

The Elves not only were first-born in Tolkien's imagination, but also first-born in his mythology of Middle-earth. They are called "First-born," or the "Elder Children," or the "Elder Race," and similar phrases. They were born of the thought of Eru, the One, and awoke by Cuiviénen, a bay of the Inland Sea of Helcar, which at the beginning of things lay far eastward in Middle-earth (neither of those place-names is mentioned in *The Lord of the Rings*). Later, Eru created Men, who are thus the "Younger Race," and so on; the two together are sometimes spoken of as the Two Kindreds.

Since High Elves, as Tolkien classifies such Elves as Elrond and Galadriel, are an idealized and elevated version of Men, we might ask what they look like. They are almost invariably tall, and handsome or comely, and have (the males anyway) strong and athletic bodies. They seem perpetually youthful (Glorfindel: "fair and young") or ageless (Elrond: "neither young nor old"). Elrond's daughter Arwen is "Young . . . and yet not so." (I, 299;*274*) Like father, like daughter, obviously. (In human terms, both are thousands of years old.) Galadriel, Arwen's grandmother, is similarly ageless; she is described as "tall . . . and beautiful, [with] hair of deepest gold. . . ." (I, 459; *419*) The beauty of wisdom and kindness within is manifested by beauty without.

But much of the beauty and character of the Elves is more hinted than shown. Seeming simplicity of outline is deceptive. The Elves have a more colored history—blacker *and* whiter, more ignoble *and* more glorious—than their calm wisdom and high demeanor in the late days of the Third Age would suggest.

Early in Book II, Gandalf conveys these checkered backgrounds within a couple of sentences as he converses with Frodo during the hobbit's recuperation at Rivendell. Speaking of the Elves of Elrond's household, and Elves in general, the wizard notes that "never *again*" will Elves consort with Sauron. (I, 294; *269;* emphasis added) He is thinking (among other things) of how Elves and the Dark Lord had seemed to cooperate in the making of the sets of Rings during the Second Age.

The Elves have shown dismaying kinds of pride and defiance at various other points in their history to be sure, as Tolkien's writings, and Gandalf's knowledge, can make clear. They had to *learn* wisdom. But to the reader of *The Lord of the Rings* their misplaced pride of craft in the matter of the Rings is probably most pertinent.

One moment later in Gandalf's conversation we get to the other extreme—a kind of apogee of Elven glory. Frodo speaks of a shining white figure he saw in the melee at the Ford of Bruinen, and Gandalf says that that was Glorfindel as the mighty Elven lord he is beyond the Sea, in Eldamar. Elves can and habitually do mute their natural splendor in Middle-earth, but those who have lived in the West can easily live in two realms, spiritually astride the limits of mere geography.

At the same time (as we will hear Legolas mention later), the Elves straddle time as well as space. All the races of Middle-earth are comparatively long-lived, but none lives long in the same sense as Elves do. I speak of Tolkien as a mythographer, or a collector and recounter of legends, in the next chapter, and of the fascination of Middle-earth's people with legends of the Elder Days. It is perhaps easy to forget that the Elves were actually there: that they were witnesses of and participants in the events of earlier ages—not just that the race of Elves existed, but that individual Elves, Elrond, Galadriel, were alive then and are alive now. In a strange way, these Elves are themselves legends.

The vicissitudes and variety of the early history of the Elves form the basis of their groupings. Elves came to life in Middle-earth, but the *Eldar* heeded the summons of the Valar and went over Sea into the West; they are known as High Elves. Those who did not heed the summons are called Lesser Elves. (These Lesser Elves and their languages hardly appear in the story.) Some Elves heard the summons indeed and began the march to the Sea but lingered in the coastlands of Middle-earth; these are known as the *Sindar* or Grey Elves. Some of the Eldar or High Elves returned again to Middle-earth, against the wishes of the Valar, and are called Exiles. These Exiles were allowed to sail yet again to the West, and some did so; but some Exiles chose to linger in Middle-earth because they loved its beauty; the Three Rings were made to preserve that loveliness. Such tarrying High Elves or Exiles are sometimes called a remnant of those who had originally been in Middle-earth.

These peregrinations make for confusion even as they suggest the deeply sundered loyalties of those Elves who love the lands on both sides of the Sea. The general Elven population of, say, Lothlórien, may be made up of Lesser Elves, but their rulers, Galadriel and Celeborn, are among the highest of the High Elves. And Legolas, of whom more anon, is a Grey Elf whose father Thranduil established his kingdom in the Woodland Realm of northern Mirkwood when it was still known as Greenwood. (Divisions of Elven languages are similarly complicated and are treated in the chapter on languages.)

This is a rather incomplete, and highly schematic, but not inaccurate account of the various sorts of Elves whom we meet in *The Lord of the Rings*.[3] They live in various places in Middle-earth:

- in Rivendell, or Imladris, or the Glen of the Cleft, also called the Last Homely House East of the Sea. Here Elrond with the help of other High Elves and Vilya, the Ring of blue stone and greatest of the Three, maintains a refuge and a meeting-place for folk from all over Middle-earth. It is here that Bilbo Baggins spends his days until it is time to leave Middle-earth altogether;
- in Lothlórien, the Golden Wood, ruled by Galadriel and her consort Celeborn (who is a great Elven lord to be sure, but of whom it has been said that he seems rather slow-witted[4]). The golden-leaved mallorn trees shelter the place, which Galadriel can preserve by the power of her Ring Nenya. Of all the Elves we meet in the tale, Galadriel is represented as perhaps the most beautiful (Éomer and Gimli argue amicably about that), and in some ways the saddest. Surely she is most conscious of actually being in exile; but she has labored unremittingly against the evil of Sauron, as, for instance, the original convener of the White Council to deal with Middle-earth's problems. Even so, she knows (and points out to Frodo) that her success will mean that she must leave the place she has worked so long to conserve. Her success, looked at more positively, will mean her acceptance by the Valar and the end of her exile;
- at the Grey Havens on the Gulf of Lune west of the Shire, the place of embarkation for the West and a place where some Elves still dwell in the late days of the Third Age;
- there are also the "Wandering Companies" of Elves whom Gildor mentions when he meets Frodo and the other hobbits in the Shire.

Finally, outside the arena of the action of *The Lord of the Rings,* Elves live in the Woodland Realm of Northern Mirkwood. This is the Realm, and these are the Elves, that Bilbo visited in *The Hobbit,* although "visited" may be a weak word for what happened to Bilbo. The King there is Thranduil, and his son Legolas is the representative of the Elves in the Company of Nine. Elrond chooses Legolas without comment, and some readers have wondered that Tolkien's creatures of ancient wisdom should be represented by an Elf who is in a sense "uninitiated" or unenhanced, rather than by a High Elf such as Glorfindel.

Elrond's choice and Tolkien's narrative logic are tenable, however. Legolas, whatever his status, is a true Elf; in the course of the journey he will be able to show us much about Elvish nature and some of the well-nigh magical ways in which it differs from mere human nature. At the same time, Legolas is a most "human" Elf: he can be playful or even boyish; he has a sense of humor; he does not have that remoteness approaching weariness or that aura of hidden power which characterizes Elrond and some of the others. He will not overawe or intimidate anyone on the journey—indeed, one of the charming touches of the tale is the unlikely friendship that springs up between the Elf Legolas and the Dwarf Gimli. Air and Earth can apparently mix successfully.

Legolas is a Silvan Elf, thus a hunter: he is a skilled archer, and like all Elves has the keenest of eyesight. As he and Gimli and Aragorn pursue the abducted Hobbits across Rohan he has no need of sustenance other than Elvish waybread or *lembas;* he has no need of rest or sleep in the ordinary human sense. This quality of endurance can hardly be called stamina, for Legolas does not even seem to approach or need to overcome tiredness. Perhaps this is because his mental and bodily clock runs at a different rate from human time; he is speaking of Lothlórien but also of himself when he says that in the perception of Elves the outer world moves quickly and slowly: quickly because the world changes faster than the Elves do; slowly because all such change is mere surface and thus unreal from the Elvish perspective, just "'ripples . . . in the . . . stream.'" (I, 503; *458*)

With all the strengths of the Elves, Legolas, their representative, has their vulnerabilities too. His particular group of Elves, the *Sindarin* or Grey Elves, heard the summons to the West but tarried on the shore of Middle-earth. Yet the call or desire of the Sea is dormant within them. This Galadriel knew. When Gandalf returns and greets his friends in Fangorn Forest, he says she sent Legolas a message: "*Beware of the Sea!*" (see II, 136; *126* for the full verse).

And the call of the Sea pursues him. So, many years later, and after having done much good work in Ithilien, Legolas builds a boat and sails westward, taking Gimli with him.

The Elves of Tolkien's imagination, as they appear (or rather, disappear) at the end of the Third Age, are a remarkable artistic achievement. He meant them to be a higher form of Men, and so they are, but with the abyssal difference that they are immortal—and their immortality gives them an unimaginably different view of life and of the world. They are never old, and they are never especially youthful either. They must have come into existence sometime and somehow, but it is difficult to suppose a baby-Elf, or a pubescent Elf; Elves just do not seem to participate in reality on such terms.

Legolas's words about time and the Elves have many bearings. Perhaps if you know you will have to endure forever, you are also unwilling to accept constant change; hence the wish of the Elves to preserve the world they have loved. Hence the Three Rings. But their Rings are bound to, and limited by the power of, the One Ring; when it is unmade so is their realm and its beauty. The wisdom of the Elves lies in knowing that, like all else, Middle-earth must change; their sadness lies in knowing that they must therefore leave it.

Thus in an odd way, the Elves are in relation to Middle-earth as readers are to *The Lord of the Rings:* they know their stay in it must end, but they deeply wish it would not. Readers are greatly advantaged, however: they are permitted to return.

Some of the terminology used in connection with Elves:

- Names for Elves in general: *Elder Children; Elder Kindred; Elder Race; Fair Folk; First-born;*
- For Elves who obeyed the Summons and crossed the Sea: *Eldar; High Elves;*
- For Eldar or High Elves who returned again to Middle-earth (disobeying orders, as it were): *Noldor;*
- For Elves who heard the Summons and began the journey but stayed on the western shore of Middle-earth: *Sindarin;*
- Many of the Sindarin eventually became known as: *Grey-Elves; Silvan Elves; Wood Elves;*
- Elves living in Lothlórien (see below) were often known as *Galadrim* (Tree-people);
- Elves of no fixed abode were referred to (at least once in the text) as Wandering Companies.

Elven Places (in each case, the commonest name is given first):

- *Grey Havens:* at the Gulf of Lune; point of embarkation from Middle-earth to the West; also called *Elf-Havens;* associated with *Círdan the Shipwright* and with *Galdor* (who was at the Council of Elrond);
- *Lothlórien:* at the juncture of the Rivers Anduin and Celebrant or *Silverlode; Dwimordene; the Golden Wood; Laurelindórinan; Lórien;* includes *Caras Galadon; Cerin Amroth;* associated with *Galadriel* and *Celeborn; Haldir* also mentioned;
- *Rivendell:* in a steep and secluded valley north of the Great East Road; on the River Bruinen just west of the Misty Mountains; *Glen of the Cleft; Imladris; Last Homely House East of the Sea;* associated with *Elrond,* his twin sons *Elladan* and *Elrohir,* his daughter *Arwen Evenstar* (or *Undomiel*), and Elf-lords like *Glorfindel;*
- *Woodland Realm:* in northern Mirkwood, the kingdom or realm of the Silvan Elves or Wood Elves; ruled by *King Thranduil,* whose son *Legolas* was a member of the Fellowship of the Ring.

Some of the terminology for lands in the West, to which Elves and some others gave allegiance or made reference (see also Chapter 2, where this information is in part duplicated):

There is a great land mass or continent in the West called *Aman.* In Westron it is also called or characterized as *the Blessed Realm, the Undying Land(s),* or *the Uttermost West* (this term usually refers to *Valinor* primarily). The western part of *Aman* is called *Valinor,* and its principal city is *Valimar;* it is the home of the Valar. A range of mountains separates this from the eastern side of Aman, where the home of the Elves is. That land is in fact on the eastern shore, facing Middle-earth, and is called *Eldamar* (in Elvish) or *Elvenhome* (in Westron). Off the shore of Elvenhome is the large island of *Tol Eressëa* or *Eressëa,* which would thus be the easternmost part of this westernmost land. It is almost certainly Eressëa that Frodo sees after he has sailed from the Grey Havens. He arrives, smells fragrances and hears singing, and in the morning, "he beheld white shores and beyond them a far green country under a swift sunrise." (III, 384; *347*)

Eleven

The Dwarves

Tolkien's Dwarves have been involved with Tolkien's Hobbits since the earliest days of his Hobbit tales, as Bilbo Baggins has rueful reason to recall. In *The Lord of the Rings* itself, some of the early signs of trouble can be detected thanks to the long acquaintanceship of Hobbits and Dwarves. In the summer before Frodo's fiftieth birthday, strange events included the news that a large number of Dwarves were moving along the old East-West Road that crossed the Shire.

Tolkien claimed that he was not strictly following Germanic or Scandinavian models for his Dwarves, but the Dwarves of Middle-earth share at least some basic characteristics with their Teutonic kindred. "The 'dwarves' of my legends are far nearer to the dwarfs of Germanic [legends] than are the Elves [to traditional European folklore] but still . . . different from them" and they are "not really Germanic 'dwarfs' and I call them 'dwarves' to mark that," he writes. Such differences as exist seem to be marked by Tolkien's use of the non-standard plural "dwarves," which I too shall use. As is often the case, Tolkien is being both traditional and original in his treatment: Gimli and his kindred are recognizably the "dwarfs" we know from folklore and folktale, but they also have characteristics that mark them as Tolkien's own "dwarves."[1]

Gimli is traditional, for example, in being short, strongly built, bearded, skilled in the use of tools (including axes), and possessed of a grim sense of humor; he is untraditional in his friendship with the Elf Legolas, and in his sworn fealty to the Elven lady Galadriel. Both sides of his nature—his tra-ditionalism and his adaptability—are shown by his loyalty: he is loyal to his forefathers and their ways; he is steadfastly loyal both to the Lady of the Golden Wood and to his friend the Silvan Elf. Gimli is thus a typical dwarf in his stamina, his strength, and his stoutness of character ("stout" I mean in the sense of "stout-hearted," not "obese," although some of Bilbo's compan-ions of years ago inclined that way). The way he shows that steadfast char-acter, in his devotion to outsiders, is what is not typical.

Clearly, Dwarves mark one of the strongest elements of continuity be-tween *The Hobbit* and *The Lord of the Rings*. But in the latter book the race of Dwarves is represented largely by Gimli Glóin, who is much more indi-vidualized than the baker's dozen of Dwarves who give Bilbo an adventure in the former. In *The Hobbit* the elder Glóin is a dwarf of middling impor-tance among the thirteen; in *The Lord of the Rings* he returns briefly as spokesman for his people at the Council of Elrond, but his son Gimli un-dertakes the perilous Quest. It is in Rivendell indeed that we learn that the Dwarves, solitary and self-sufficient people as they are, are involved in the general troubles of Middle-earth and in the general diminution that marks the end of the Third Age: old Glóin tells Frodo that in some fields, like min-ing, Dwarvish skill is superior today; in others, the arts of the Dwarves are sadly lacking. One of Gimli's joyful tasks after the War of the Rings will be to restore for a while at least some of the Dwarf crafts of old.

Like all the major characters of the tale, Gimli speaks Westron, the com-mon tongue of Middle-earth, which Tolkien renders as English. But his own language is difficult and closely held; few outsiders can learn it (Gandalf ap-parently did) and it occurs in the world only in a phrase or two or in a few place-names like Khazad-dûm, for Moria. Most secret of all are the Dwarves' own names, spoken only among themselves. On the Rumpelstiltskin theory of information, the Dwarves do not allow others the power over them that knowing their real names might confer. The names by which we know Dwarves (Gimli, Dwalin, and so on) are all Northern, Mannish; in our world's frame of reference they are Old Norse or Icelandic.

We may suppose that like all Dwarves, Gimli is a craftsman, or metal-smith, or perhaps a stoneworker of great skill (actually I do not recall

Tolkien's mentioning a specific "specialty" for Gimli). It is indeed the work of the Dwarves and the resulting artifacts that figure largely in *The Lord of the Rings* and link that tale up strongly with *The Hobbit:* it was on his travels with the Dwarves that Bilbo acquired both Sting, his Orc-sensitive sword, and the mithril coat (presented by the Dwarves), which is worn as armor. Both these treasures he bestows on Frodo as the Company leaves Rivendell; both prove valuable to the fulfillment of the Quest.

Gimli is unmarried, we may suppose, for a great many Dwarves never do marry. The proportion of females among the Dwarf population is about one in three and even with this shortfall, marriage is not inevitable even for the women. Some females choose not to wed; some males are devoted to their craft to the exclusion of domesticity. Female Dwarves seldom appear in the outer world, and they dress as males when they do. Under these conditions, the whole question of the survival of the race of Dwarves is highly problematical.[2]

One trait that Tolkien's Dwarves share to some extent with the dwarfs of this world, so to say, is greed. Greed formed part of the motive for the quest into which Bilbo found himself dragooned; greed provided both the dangers lurking in the Mines of Moria (delving too deep for *mithril,* the Dwarves awakened the Balrog) and the motive for the return of Balin and others (some three decades before the events in *The Lord of the Rings*) in spite of these known dangers. Because Dwarvish greed is very real, Galadriel is able to confer a boon upon Gimli Glóin as the Company leaves Lothlórien: besides the strand of her hair he requested, she gives him a conditional promise "'that your hands shall flow with gold, and yet over you gold shall have no dominion.'" (I, 487; *444*)

Gimli's exploits are but the most recent in Dwarvish history in the Third Age: earlier significant events include the death of Thorin in Moria in 2790, the events recounted in *The Hobbit* (2941–2), the re-entry of Balin and other Dwarves into Moria in 2989, and their being slain there five years later.

Somewhere back in that history is the question of the relations between Dwarves and Elves. For readers of *The Lord of the Rings,* one of its most intriguing features is the quite evident enmity, or at the best of times wary neutrality, between these two folk. Tolkien makes the existence of that dislike very clear (as in Gimli's humiliation at the borders of Lothlórien) without making entirely clear its reasons. They are grounded in both recent history and in the very creation of the world.

Ilúvatar, the One, Eru, was the Creator. He created first of all great but not omnipotent beings whom Middle-earth folk know as the Valar (or maybe "gods"). His creative designs also included what are called the Children of Ilúvatar: the First-born or Elves, and the Second-born or Men.

But one of the Valar, Aulë, who was a smith or craftsman (somewhat analogous, I suppose, in the pantheon of Middle-earth to the Classical Vulcan or Hæphestus) was eager to teach, and so created and brought to life beings unauthorized by Ilúvatar, and made stone-hard. Ilúvatar chided Aulë severely for this usurpation of power, but Aulë pleaded high purpose and good intention. Ilúvatar had compassion on Aulë and his worthy but mistaken aims, and let his creatures live, and they became the Dwarves (thus does intention structure result, as has been mentioned). They were not allowed to wake before the First-born awoke, but there was nonetheless a sense of hostility from the beginning between Elf and Dwarf because the latter, the Children of Aulë, had as it were intervened, or been interposed, in the unfolding of Ilúvatar's creation.[3]

Stories such as these are what Tolkien calls elf-legends, of course. Tolkien's stance toward his material is not only that of a historian or chronicler, but sometimes also that of mythographer, and that is especially true in *The Silmarillion*. It is often a question of tact to decide which Tolkien we are reading at a given moment, for as a writer he adopts many roles: in *The Hobbit* a teller of children's tales somewhat like Kenneth Grahame or Beatrix Potter; in *The Lord of the Rings* a craftsman of fiction with much historical and scholarly depth, somewhat like Sir Walter Scott; in *The Silmarillion* a compiler of ancient story somewhat like Thomas Bulfinch. The important word in all three comparisons is "somewhat."

And from the point of view of the inhabitants of Middle-earth, the stories of the Elder Days (the First Age) are indeed legend. No one who has access to them—Aragorn, Gimli, even Frodo and Sam—tires of recounting them. In a world being battered by war and evil they provide continuity, and imaginative riches, and solace.

Later in the First Age Elves and Dwarves quarreled over the proper setting of the jewels the Silmarils, and their ownership: without reference to this particular dispute, Gimli celebrates the wealth and greatness of the Dwarves in olden times as he chants in Moria of how "'*The world was fair in Durin's day.*'" (I, 411; *376–7*)

But for the terrible events that take place within the Mines of Moria, the bickering between Dwarf and Elf, with its long background, might have continued indefinitely. As it is, everyone leaves Moria chastened and comes to Galadriel's land, where she can act as a healer. When Gimli experiences her kindness and understanding (to say nothing of her beauty), Galadriel wins a heart for life.

Thus it is both excellent and remarkable that the son of that Elven king in whose hall Thorin Oakenshield had been held, and the distant cousin of that same Thorin, should become fast friends in the course of the adventures of the Ring. But as with so much else in Middle-earth, it is too late: the Age of Men is upon them.

Yet in the course of the campaign against evil in the late days of the Third Age, Gimli son of Glóin has two profound experiences of Dwarf culture. In the first he must look back on the fate of his people and what has been lost; in the other he must look forward to their future and what can be gained. In Moria Gimli undergoes deep loss and sadness at cultural failure; in Aglarond he feels great hope for the last and perhaps highest achievement of his people.

Unlike the other members of the Company of Nine, who dread entering Moria for a variety of good reasons, Gimli looks forward to seeing his people's old stronghold again. To Sam's rather tactless remark about the "darksome holes" that constitute Moria, Gimli replies with indignant pride that "'These are not holes. . . . This is the great realm and city of the Dwarrowdelf.'" (I, 411; *376*) But when the party comes to the tomb of Balin and reads the sad record of the Book of Mazarbul, they recognize that the Dwarves' attempt of three decades ago to re-colonize Moria was a failure. Gimli can only grieve in the stoical silence of a Dwarf.

Yet, stout and stubborn as he is, Gimli persists and does his deeds in the War of the Rings. (The Paths of the Dead daunt even him, however; unlike Moria or Aglarond they were not fashioned by Dwarf-craft—they are as alien to him as to any surface dweller. But it is a measure of the strong dread the Paths inspire, not of any want of courage in Gimli, that he finds himself almost faint with fear as the Grey Company follows Aragorn through the Gate of the Dead. He goes in nonetheless.)

That horror past, Gimli continues to bear his part. Even though the Age of Men can be said to have officially begun with the departure of Elrond from Middle-earth in the autumn of 3021 T. A., or even with the old-style New Year's Day of that year, March 25, much of the aura of the Third Age will linger as long as Aragorn, now Elessar or Telcontar, sits on the throne of the Reunited Kingdom; like his liege prince Faramir, Aragorn has indeed the "wisdom and sadness of the Elder Race," and under his rule Gimli and Legolas can do much good work. Legolas brings his people to Faramir's realm of Ithilien and helps to restore it as the garden of Gondor. Gimli turns his attention to Aglarond.

The Glittering Caves, like so much else that enriches *The Lord of the Rings,* are completely unnecessary to the immediate story. But there they are. In the later phases of the Battle of Helm's Deep, Legolas asks Aragorn where Gimli is. Aragorn says that he does not know, but that the Dwarf can look after himself; maybe, Aragorn suggests, he is in the caves behind the stronghold; he would enjoy them.

Indeed he does. After the battle, Gimli speaks of Aglarond in the bravura language of a Dwarf poet; he derides the notion that "caves" is an adequate word (I select only a few rhapsodic phrases): the caves are "'vast and beautiful'"; the walls gleam with "'precious ore'"; "'folded marble'" shows "'white'" "'saffron'" "'dawn-rose'" draped like "'frozen clouds.'" (II, 193–4; *179–80*)

Gimli's paean goes on through four substantial paragraphs, and this, he resolves, is to be his work and that of his fellow Dwarves from the Lonely Mountains: not to mine or extract from this lovely place, but to refine and heighten and display to the world its beauty, carefully and artfully.

In the last chapter of the narrative proper, "The Grey Havens," Tolkien makes clear what the Elves will be leaving behind in Middle-earth—their memory and their heritage will long be preserved in the beauty of the Shire's gardens and in the great mallorn tree that stands in the Party Field. By contrast, what memorial the Dwarves can create for themselves is not set out as plainly in the body of the text, but is clearly implied here and in the Appendices. Gimli will become Lord of the Glittering Caves, and the deep tragedy of Moria will in some measure be redeemed.

Gandalf had told Gimli to take the Book of Mazarbul with him as they proceeded through the Mines (see I, 419; *383*), so perhaps the book is preserved in some Dwarvish archive somewhere to remind the Dwarves of the high price of greed, just as Aglarond may remind them that beauty is priceless.

Twelve

THE ENTS

A lthough stories of talking trees are not unfamiliar in fairy tale and fantasy literature, Tolkien's tree-creatures or Ents are among his most original inventions. Yet they were *not* an invention if that means the end result of a process of thought. Rather, like Faramir, they were something of a surprise: "I did not consciously invent them," he told W. H. Auden, and to another inquirer he wrote that the Ents "only presented themselves to my sight, without premeditation or any previous knowledge . . ."[1] when he came to a crucial point in Book III.

As Tolkien can describe how the moment of creation (or discovery) of the Ents came without authorial effort, we can also discover in some detail the places, literary and imaginative, where the Ents originated.

They originated, pretty obviously, in Tolkien's love of trees. Tolkien's short story "Leaf by Niggle," which is about an artist struggling to finish a major work, and which to that extent bears upon the efforts expended on *The Lord of the Rings,* is also about trees. More specifically, as Tolkien recounts in the foreword to *Tree and Leaf* and elsewhere, it was inspired by a tree: a large poplar that stood near his house and that he loved; it had been lopped and was threatened with being cut down entirely, an act that Tolkien as a tree lover deplored and sought to prevent.

Tolkien is certainly an advocate for trees, but the Ents originated in Tolkien's love for language as well as in his tree-love. To Kathleen Farrer in

1954 (soon after *The Two Towers* came out) he wrote that the Ents "grew rather out of their name, than the other way around. I always thought that something ought to be done about the peculiar A. Saxon word *ent* for a 'giant.' . . ."[2] In the letter to Auden already mentioned he said that "Ents are composed of philology, literature, and life. . . ." They partly came, for instance, from his schoolboy unhappiness "with the shabby use made in Shakespeare of the coming of 'Great Birnam wood to high Dunsinane hill.'"[3]

The editors of Tolkien's letters annotate the Anglo-Saxon as coming from the Old English poem *The Wanderer*, l. 87: "'*eald enta geweorc idlu stodon*', 'the old work of giants [i.e., ancient buildings, erected by a former race] stood desolate.'"[4] The Shakespeare reference is to *Macbeth* 4.1.93.

Readers rejoice with Tolkien at the sudden inspiration that brought the Ents into the story, and perhaps react with awe and wonder as do Merry and Pippin when Treebeard comes upon them, but the inspiration created problems, which Tolkien recognized: for example, the conflict between the agelessness of Tom Bombadil and the vast age of Treebeard. Tolkien notes that Ents did not exist in his earlier tales, but "since Treebeard [knows of] Beleriand [sunk under the Sea at the end of the First Age] they will have to come in."[5]

Of equal interest to the seeming conflict in assigned seniority is how Tolkien imagined fitting the Ents into the framework of Middle-earth itself, within the dispensation of its Creating powers: "No one," he writes, "knew whence they (Ents) came or first appeared." But some High Elves such as Galadriel believed that one of the Valar asked Eru, the One, to fashion a response to the creation of Dwarves, requesting that He "give life to things made of living things not stone," and the tree-creatures or Ents were the result.[6]

The passage from which these words were taken was a pencilled note to a draft of a letter: it may represent only Tolkien's preliminary thinking about how to retrofit the Ents into his earlier accounts of Middle-earth. What he proposes is consistent, however: the Oromë to whom the male Ents are devoted is the Vala also known as "Tauron," the Lord of the Forest.

Still another matter we need to understand about the Ents is that for all the suddenness of their eruption into Tolkien's imagination, the Ents occupy a well-realized place in his world. Tolkien has not made all the connections he would perhaps want to (with, say, Tom Bombadil), but Treebeard is very much aware of the pernicious activities of his neighbor Saruman and of Saruman's Orcs; his relations with Elves go back to the very beginnings of Entish consciousness (Elves taught Ents speech), and so on. It is, however, quite fitting that Treebeard has never heard of Hobbits and needs to add a line to his lists. They are comparative late-comers to the socio-political world of Middle-earth, and are in any case not a woodsy folk.

At any rate, Treebeard offers his own giant-scale brand of hospitality to the two hobbits: he takes them to his cave of Wellinghall; he gives them refreshing drink (which eventually enables Merry and Pippin to become among the tallest hobbits ever known); he gives them grassy beds to sleep on. Again, the pattern of danger and violence, followed by rest and refreshment (in the inimitable manner of Fangorn) is observable here. Counsel is taken, although this time the hobbits have advice, or at least information, to offer that will change the course of the War of the Rings.

For, concentrating on self only, wrapped up in self, the forces of evil— mostly Saruman's forces, in this case—have made the mistake of thinking the Ents negligible. Had he reflected, the wizard probably would not have sent Orcs with axes into Fangorn, but wrapped up in his own designs, or perhaps in Sauron's, Saruman has forgotten, if he ever knew, the true nature of Ents—the long passivity, the slowness to anger, and the fierceness of anger once kindled. The heat of the Ents' anger, and their great physical and moral power, explode Saruman's little dream of making himself into a Power, as Treebeard puts it. (II, 96; *90*)

After all, the Ents have nothing to lose, for the ways of male and female Ents have long since parted. And that brings up the question about Ents that has always concerned readers most: What has happened to the Entwives?

Treebeard explains it all to Merry and Pippin at considerable length (which is in the nature of all Entish explanations), and he stresses that the Entwives did not *die* but that the Ents had lost them. Their ways diverged: the Ents were wanderers in the forest, the Entwives were gardeners in the fields. The Entwives cultivated their gardens on the other side of the River Anduin and when the Ents went to visit they found desolation. War had scorched their earth, and the Entwives were gone; the regions where their gardens had been are now called the Brown Lands. Some said they had seen the Entwives going east, or west, or south, but according to Treebeard they could not be found. (see II, 100; *93*)

Tolkien's own view of the fate of the Entwives wavered somewhat: he told Naomi Mitchison in 1954, "I think that . . . the Entwives [were] destroyed . . . in the War of the Last Alliance."[7] Almost two decades later, in 1972, he answered the query, "did the Ents ever find the Entwives?" with a different sort of certainty: "it is plain that there would be for Ents no reunion in 'history'. . . ."[8] "Thus Tolkien echoes Treebeard's own bittersweet thought that there might be some meeting sometime, but it "'will only be when we have both lost all that we now have.'" (II, 100; *94*)

So the War of the Rings marks (though it does not cause) the passing of the Ents, valiant and vital as their part in it is. The absence of the Entwives betokens inevitable reproductive failure (there do seem to be younger Ents around, but there have been no Entings for many years), and the diminution of forests in Middle-earth may well mean the end of the work of the Ents. Both Elrond and Treebeard, speaking of such woodlands as the Old Forest and Fangorn Forest, say that these are but remnants of great forestlands that once stretched across Middle-earth. You might think that deforestation would imply population increase, the clearing of lands for fields to till or settlements to build. That may perhaps have been true in the early days of the Third Age, but now the empty lands so often spoken of by Aragorn and others are, sadly, empty of trees as well as all else.

Closely related to the Ents, and vital to the success of the first phase of the War of the Rings, are the Huorns, which, since they have only a limited voice in the story, are little understood. Legolas, a Wood-Elf ever sympathetic to things arboreal, says of the forest before Helm's Deep, "'These are the strangest trees that ever I saw.'" He wishes to talk to them, for "'in time I might come to understand'" them. (II, 193; *178*)

The Orcs attacking Helm's Deep are caught between its walls and defenders at their front, and the forest of Huorns at their back. Merry saw the Huorns leave the vicinity of Isengard, as he later tells Aragorn and the others, and he goes on to say more about the nature of these creatures: "'. . . I think they are Ents that have become almost like trees, at least to look at . . . [but] they still have voices and can speak with the Ents. . . .'" (II, 217; *200*)

There is therefore in the Fangorn world a kind of hierarchy, headed by such "true Ents" as Treebeard himself, the eldest and wisest of all such beings. He has two near-contemporaries, but Finglas, or Leaflock, has become almost tree-ish, and Fladrif, or Skinbark, has exiled himself to the high hills. So Fangorn or Treebeard stands alone among such younger Ents as Quickbeam. Some Ents are continually getting tree-ish, as he tells Merry and Pippin, and some trees are getting almost Entish. (II, 89; *83*) Below "true Ents" are the reversionary, the atavistic Huorns. And finally there are the trees themselves, which are the vast majority of the population of forests throughout Middle-earth.

Last, it should be asked whether the odd sight reported by Sam's cousin Hal in the Shire's Northfarthing, of a tree-like "giant" stalking about, does in fact link up with Treebeard and Fangorn Forest (see I, 73; *68*). Treebeard has said that the Ents searched for the Entwives, who were said to have gone east or west or south; no one mentioned north (the direction of the Shire). But surely if an Ent had been out scouting, Treebeard of all folk would have known about it. As it is, when Merry and Pippin are describing the Shire to Treebeard, he says "an odd thing": "'you never see any, hm, any Ents round there, do you?'" (II, 94; *88*). It is a tiny but tantalizing disconnect.[9]

Another feature of the rather incomplete treatment of the Ents is that we see very little of them beyond Book III. At Isengard, after his coronation, Aragorn gives them the freedom of the realm, but Treebeard sees little use in that privilege since his is a dying race. Galadriel and Celeborn, old friends of Ents, affirm that Ents and Elves shall probably not meet again anywhere in Middle-earth. As an Ent, though, Treebeard's nature is essentially cheerful; he drains a bowl of ent-draught with Merry and Pippin and his last words remind them to send any news of Entwives that they may hear.

Whatever the gaps in the Ents' story, we ought once again to be grateful that there is so much in Middle-earth that is ancient. Ancient evils like the Balrog and Shelob bring terror and suspense; ancient forces for good like Tom Bombadil and Treebeard bring comfort and hope. But like Tom, Treebeard in these last days of the Third Age has chosen to withdraw into his own realm, to tend to his own charges, and not to establish links with other groups or other communities until historical emergency forces him to act.

Still, Ents belong among the finest and oldest things in Tolkien's world, even though his creative conception of them may have been (comparatively) late and abrupt.

In Treebeard's own view of the organization of things in Middle-earth, Ents belong somewhere between Elves and Men: they are less selfish and more empathetic than Men, but more adaptable and changeable than Elves, "'for they are steadier and keep their minds on things longer,'" as Treebeard tells the hobbits. (II, 89; *84*) Ents are betwixt and between: Elves take long views and do not die; Men take short views and do die; Ents live long lives but must die. Or, put another way, given these traits: Elves are past-oriented, Men are future-oriented, and Ents are present-oriented.

You can see that difference by looking at one of Tolkien's favorite devices of characterization: his people's eyes. Frodo first sees Elrond in his House at Rivendell and thinks his eyes are twilight gray (see I, 299; *274*), that is, cool, clear, remote. Treebeard's deep brown eyes on the other hand impress Pippin with great depths of memory to be sure, "but their surface was sparkling with the present. . . ." (II, 83; *78*)

Indeed, the eyes of Merry and Pippin's "young" Ent-friend Quickbeam are shining with the light of battle as the Ents break up their conclave, their Ent-moot, and prepare to move on Isengard. And in the eyes of Treebeard is also sadness, for he knows, and tells the hobbits, that it may well be the last march of the Ents: sadness for his people perhaps, but no personal unhappiness, for Treebeard knows too that they march to deal evil a devastating blow.

Thirteen

HUMANKIND

Tolkien was brought up in an older world; born in 1892, he spent much of his childhood in what was even then a backwater. This background is significant in several ways, not least in how he uses language. When he speaks of "Men" he is using the masculine form as the generic form, to include all human beings. This is a dated usage now, of course; but it must also be noted that in a Middle-earth of constant war, danger, and travel and adventure, most of the characters we meet are indeed male. So, for better or worse, "Men" has a basis in fact as well as custom.

Taking the term neutrally, though, to mean all human beings, the Fourth Age of Middle-earth is to be the Age of Men. All other sentient races will have departed or sunk from sight. In saying that our present is in a certain sense Middle-earth's future, we have to stress applicability, not allegory. Thus it is useful to see what place Men occupied in Middle-earth in the Third Age.[1]

C. S. Lewis was Tolkien's good friend and Oxford colleague for many years; as fellow members of the Inklings they met weekly at a pub and heard each other's works in progress. In Lewis's quasi–science fiction novel, *Out of the Silent Planet,* the hero, Ransom (said to be modeled in part on Tolkien), goes to Mars, where he encounters several races or species of intelligent beings. When he describes Earth to them, they lament the fact that we have only one kind of intelligent being. "'Your thought must be at the mercy of your blood'" one says. "'For you cannot compare it with thought that floats on a different blood.'"[2]

That is the case in the world as we now have it. But in the Third Age of Middle-earth, Tolkien's Men live in a world with at least three other races or species of intelligent creatures: Elves, Dwarves, and Ents. The Hobbits are a special class of humans, Tolkien says, but they still seem different enough to merit some individual consideration: the Little People contrasted with the Big People perhaps, as at Bree. And this list does not include the parody forms of the other races, such as Orcs. So "Men" live among several different "bloods."

All these races have aspects of the human, of course; they would otherwise be unrecognizable and repulsive: but what of those *represented* as human?

Men are not the *eldest* intelligent race. Elves are the First-born, the Elder Children of Ilúvatar. Even Dwarves have an unofficial kind of priority, and Ents too are very ancient, although Tolkien had not yet found a place for them in his creation myths.

Men are not the *most* intelligent race—for wisdom one would have to go to the Elves with their long views of existence and their hard-earned insights. Gandalf the wizard is of course no Man; he only assumes that form; he is in fact a being of angelic nature from the other side of the Sea.

Clearly in the Third Age of Middle-earth Men have very few natural advantages. To explain some of what follows, Faramir, son of Denethor, has become the natural spokesman; he tells Frodo a great deal about his city and his own people and thus about the character and history of the race of Men. I suppose in a way Tolkien has split himself up as a Man writing about Men: he has said he is a Hobbit in all but size—and he is, in his love of the ordinary, of creature comforts, of home. But Tolkien has also said that the character most like himself is Faramir, adding that he lacks what Faramir has and Frodo finds—courage.[3] He is like Faramir perhaps in his idealism, in his love of learning, and in his taking long perspectives on events.

One of the disadvantages Men have, from their own point of view, is that they must die. As mentioned in the chapter on Elves, the great impassable barrier between Man and Elf is Man's mortality. In his brief account of the fortunes of Númenor in the Second Age, Tolkien tells us that in that great island kingdom (his obvious analogue of Atlantis), Men, though endowed with extraordinarily long lives, were forbidden by the Valar to seek immortality. They had to die "since the Valar were not permitted to take from them the Gift of Men (or the Doom of Men, as it was afterwards called)." (III, 390; *352*) This clause is packed full of meaning: the passive verb affirms again the existence of a power higher than the Valar; it also holds the idea that death ought to be regarded as a boon. This is the concept that some of the Men of Númenor could not grasp.

The hunger to live forever led some Númenoreans to disobey the Valar and invade the Undying Lands, seeking to wrest immortality into their own hands. For their rebellious presumption they were destroyed, and Númenor was sunk beneath the Western Sea. The loyal Númenoreans, who did not rebel, were allowed to escape to Middle-earth and there founded the kingdoms of Men that came to be known as Arnor, in the north, and Gondor, in the south. (This information, and much more, is in Appendices A and B of Part III of *The Lord of the Rings*.)

The histories show us how there are close affinities between the descendants of the Men of the West (Aragorn and the other Rangers, Faramir, Imrahil of Dol Amroth, for instance) and Elves, not just in blood, although those ties exist, but also in moral probity and nobility of demeanor. The Man-Elf links were once much closer still, as Faramir tells Frodo that in early days, Men "'fought beside the Elves. . . .'" (II, 365; *340*) But eventually Men and Elves began to go their separate ways, thanks to time, forgetfulness, and, in no small part, the machinations of Sauron. In Faramir's Gondor, however, the bonds between Elves and Men, though weakened, remain as real as anywhere in Middle-earth.

But human hunger for the unattainable, for the evanescent, and for the actually harmful has been part of the story of Men throughout their stay in Middle-earth, as we shall further see. Even the Númenoreans who did not rebel and who came to Middle-earth after Númenor's fall were obsessed with evading death, and thus with death itself. Faramir explains to Frodo that "'Death was ever present,'" for rulers and scholars from Númenor craved endless life. (II, 363; *338*) They put astrology, and alchemy, and medicine to work seeking it. They honored dead ancestors and neglected living heirs, until at last there was no heir, and the throne of Gondor stood empty.

The irony of all this is inescapable: seeking to live forever, these Men neglected to live at all. Seeking to prolong life, they failed to nourish it.

Each race—Elves and Men—perhaps envies the other for what it does not have: Legolas hears in the language of Rohan "'the sadness of Mortal Men'" (II, 142; *132*), while Pippin sees in at least one countenance the "sadness of the Elder Race." (III, 101; *91*) Do Elves suppose we (Men) are sad because we know we must die? Do we (Men) suppose Elves are sad because they know they cannot die?

In the beginning it was Eru's plan that the First-born, the Elder Children, Elves, should remain in the world as long as the world lasted, tens of thousands of centuries if it came to that. But the Younger Children, Men, should remain in the world for only a stated interval, and then depart it was known not where. Part of the evil of the Enemy's schemes was to teach Men to regard this departure, called Death, with fear and hatred.

In the early days of Middle-earth there were three Houses of Men—the House of Beor, the House of Haleth, and the House of Hador; all were in varying degrees friendly with the Elves. These Houses (leading families, clans, dynasties even) were the foundational units of Men in Middle-earth, legendarily and genealogically. The Three Houses are not mentioned as such in the body of *The Lord of the Rings,* but again Faramir can elucidate some aspects of the matter. (In spite of his claim to be unlearned, Faramir is full of information—perhaps he is interested because he himself harks back to the nobler Men of old; perhaps because he was once Gandalf's pupil. In any case he sometimes seems to speak for Tolkien himself.)

From the Three Houses of Men have come what Faramir calls the Three Kindreds of Men, a term describing the present orders of Men as he sees them in Middle-earth at the close of the Third Age. As is true of the Elves and even the Ents, a term like the "Three Kindreds" describes for Men a ranking, status, class order, or historical situation.

Faramir tells Frodo that his people call Men "'High, or Men of the West [from Númenor] . . . Middle Peoples, Men of the Twilight [Men of Rohan, for instance] . . . and the Wild, the Men of Darkness.'" (II, 364; *339*)

Yet such is the decline of things here in the last days of the Third Age that the High, represented by the Men of Gondor, for example, have become more like Middle Men; even while the Men of Rohan have, by association, become more Gondorean. Or so says Faramir, and his evidence is that in Gondor they now love war for itself, and to be a warrior is the highest calling, and thus was Boromir, his brother, reckoned the greatest Man of the realm (see III, 364; *339*).

So Faramir may represent a throwback to the nobler Men of Númenor, but Boromir represents an aspect of Man as he has become.

Boromir the war-lover believes in the superiority of Men; it would not be a great exaggeration to say that he is contemptuous of other races. When he tries to seize the Ring from Frodo at Amon Hen, he wheedles the hobbit: Why should we not use the Ring? he asks. Others might be harmed by the Ring: "'*But each to his own kind*. . . . Men . . . will not be corrupted. . . . The Ring would give me power of Command. . . . and all men would flock to my banner!'" (I, 515; *468–9;* emphasis added)

When Frodo remains unpersuaded by these arguments, Boromir grows angry and imperious: the Ring "'should be mine. Give it to me!'" (I, 516; *470*)

Boromir soon repents of his madness, but as Paul Kocher observes, "In this context, Boromir's saying 'Each to his own kind' is in effect a proclamation of the superiority of Men over other species, of Gondoreans over other men, of . . . Boromir over other Gondoreans."[4] A sense of the superiority of one's own kind to the detriment of other kinds, often expressed as mistrust, infects Middle-earth. One of Aragorn's major tasks when he assumes the throne will be to rebuild mutual respect.

And it is to be hoped that Aragorn is more nearly representative of Men than Boromir was. And it seems likely: if a Hobbit is a clod with a hero asleep inside him, Aragorn is a hero with a king asleep inside him.[5] He will be king in the highest sense of the word, not just head man, or arbitrary authority, but an epitome of his people, a distillation of his people's, Men's, best qualities.

For in spite of Boromir's unfortunate lapse (which he soon redeems after all) there still is hope for Men, self-regarding as they might be, in these latter days. The best hope for eventual peace and order in a world of several intelligent species is mutual respect, and amid the nearly empty lands of Middle-earth, a few examples can still be found.

One might, for instance, consider Bree. There Men and Hobbits (the Big Folk and the Little Folk, both called human but widely different) live side by side, each kind believing itself essential to the community. *"Nowhere else in the world"* did this happy situation exist, Tolkien tells us. (I, 206; *189;* emphasis added)

One might also consider the Wild Men or Woses of the Stonewain Valley. They are "'Remnants of an older time,'" as Elfhelm tells Merry (III, 128; *115*); they are the very image of the old Púkel-men Merry saw in Dunharrow. When Éomer of Rohan questions their old chief's information, he replies in surly tones that "'Wild Men are wild, free, but not children. . . .'" and goes on to demand that his people be left unharassed after the war. (III, 130–31; *116–17*) The demand for respect can hardly be clearer than that, and the Men of Rohan will honor it.

One other tiny but poignant instance of respect—indeed, compassion—(Hobbit for Man, this time) comes to mind. "'[C]urse the Southrons!'" Damrod has cried (II, 338; *315*) as he and his fellow Rangers of Ithilien prepare to battle the swarthy exotic invaders—paynim-like or saracen-like, as they seem to be—from Harad far to the southeast. Sam Gamgee watches the ambush from hiding as one of the foreigners is killed; his body rolls to a stop a few feet from Sam: "He wondered what the man's name was and where he came from. . . ." (II, 341; *317*) He wondered if the man had volunteered or had somehow been conscripted or cajoled into fighting so far from his native country; and whether he would just rather have stayed at home. Sam has to wonder what prompts a battle of Men against Men and whether even Men would not prefer peace. Sam has a measure of imaginative sympathy for the unfortunate outlander lying dead near him, like Sam a stranger and afraid in a world he never made.

If Faramir and Aragorn can exemplify the high ideals to which Men can aspire, Sam and Frodo (Hobbits though they are) can exemplify the simpler human virtues Men might live by. In any case, what is regretted here in the late days of the Third Age is not Man himself as chief occupant-to-be of Middle-earth, but the loss of variety and plenitude. Man is not bad per se but much else that is good must be given up. There is optimism in

The Lord of the Rings, there is the providential and the near-miraculous, there is victory. There is also, however, elegy, and loss, and the encroachment of drabness.

Finally, though, what seems to be characteristic of Men as Men is not so much their good or evil, or their triumphs, as their mere persistence. One of the more memorable passages in the story about *us,* so to speak, is a conversation between a Dwarf and an Elf (unbiased observers, surely) talking of "Men." Gimli Glóin is admiring Gondor's buildings, noting that the oldest are the best built. He says that Men begin well but "'they fail of their promise.'" But Men do persist, Legolas returns, and in the end, "'The deeds of Men will outlast us, Gimli.'" (III, 182; *164*)

If we are supposed to consider Hobbits as a special kind of Men or human beings, as Tolkien tells us, how do they fit into all this?

The answer to that is, not very well. Tolkien gave us a great deal of information about Hobbits before his tale began, and we learn much more (about their—or at least Frodo's—craving for mushrooms, about the seed of courage, often well concealed, in the heart of each Hobbit, and the like) as the story proceeds. What the story really brings out is that the differences between ordinary Men (Big Folk, as they say at Bree) and Hobbits are more significant than the similarities, and both kinds see those differences more clearly than the likenesses. Boromir is not talking about Hobbits considered as Men when he is talking about how Men should have the Ring—he is trying to take it away from a Hobbit, after all. Sam is not thinking about how much alike Men and Hobbits are when he sees the Southron fall—it is his first view, we are told, "of a battle of Men against Men, and he did not like it much." (II, 340–1; *317*)

Or again, riding with Gandalf, Pippin arrives at the Gates of Minas Tirith and Gandalf introduces him as "'Peregrin, a very valiant man.'" At this Pippin speaks up indignantly, "'Man! Indeed not! I am a hobbit and no more valiant than I am a man. . . . '" (III, 21; *21*) If there were taxonomists in Middle-earth, Hobbits might be classified as Men, but culturally and in most other important ways, they consider themselves quite distinct from those larger, clumsier beings.

In another example of Hobbit relations to Men, when the Hobbits return to their beloved Shire after the Ring has been destroyed, they find it run by Men (with the compliance of a few weak-willed Hobbits). The opposition that the historical situation has set up between Men and Hobbits can hardly be clearer than here. In what comes to be called the Battle of Bywater the reckoning is plain: 70 Men ("ruffians") and 19 Hobbits are killed.

Thus we have to believe that the harmonious situation of the Big Folk and the Little Folk at Bree, described as Frodo and his friends set out, was not only exceptional but impermanent. Overall the Big Folk will dominate, and the Little Folk, the Hobbits, will be marginalized, as contemporary phrase has it. Even in his Prologue Tolkien emphasizes both the difference and the dwindling when he tells us that Hobbits "avoid us with dismay" and that they have skillfully developed "the art of disappearing swiftly and silently. . . ." (I, 19–20; *19–20*) It seems a pity, especially if we are to suppose that the homely and simple virtues that the Hobbits embody (limited as they may be in some ways) are also disappearing.

These are the Men of Middle-earth, according to Faramir's classification of the Three Kindreds:

HIGH, OR MEN OF THE WEST (Dúnedain: "Dún-Edain" = "West-Men")

- Rangers of the North (remnants of the lost kingdom of Arnor in the North, including or especially Aragorn)
- Men of Gondor (Faramir himself would be an excellent example; Boromir had less of that high demeanor; Prince Imrahil of Dol Amroth, who helped greatly in the defense of Minas Tirith, is of this ancestry)

MIDDLE PEOPLES, OR MEN OF THE TWILIGHT

- the Rohirrim, the Men of Rohan

- the Hobbits (if they are "Men" at all—see the discussion above—they would belong in this group because of their northern background)
- others still living in the North: these could include the Men of Dale and the Men of Esgaroth on the Long Lake, whom Bilbo met in *The Hobbit*
- others who sent or brought aid to defend Minas Tirith:
  > Forlong the Fat, Lord of Lossarnoch and his Men
  > Dervorin of Ringló Vale
  > Duinhir and his sons Duilin and Derufin from Morthrond, the Blackroot Vale
  > Golasgil of Anfalas
  > Hirluin the Fair of the Green Hills from Pennath Gelin

(Yet, given the close relationship between Númenor as it was and Gondor as it came to be, at least some of these Men just named were doubtless of the Dúnedain or Men of the West. For a more complete census of those sending aid to Minas Tirith, see III, 49; *46*.)

THE WILD, MEN OF DARKNESS
(Despite the service of some of these groups to Sauron, "Men of Darkness" here does not mean evil, only "unenlightened")

- black men out of Far Harad (mentioned at the Battle of the Pelennor Fields only)
- Corsairs of Umbar
- Easterlings
- Men of Bree
- Men of Dunland (Dunlendings: see more in the chapter on languages)
- Men of Harad (Harardrim)
- Southrons (a generic term for several groups)
- Variags of Khand (mentioned at Pelennor Fields only)
- Woses of the Stonewain Valley

Some of the terminology used in connection with "Men":

As might be expected, given their diversity, there are more names for Men than for any other group in Middle-earth. Many are given in the three-fold classification cited just above.

- Many terms exist by analogy with nomenclature for Elves (see above): *Followers, Second-born, Younger Children,* etc.
- Many terms are purely geographic or locational designations: *Men of Dale.*
- Some suggest both origin and status: *Men of Westernesse.*
- A single group may have a multiplicity of designations (which should surprise no one) e. g., *Eorlings, Éothéod, Horse-boys* (term used derisively by Orcs), *Horse Folk, Masters of Horses, Men of the Mark, Men of the Rid-dermark, Men of Rohan, Riders of Rohan,* the *Rohirrim, Sons of Eorl, Whiteskins* (another derisive Orc term)—all labels for the skilled blond horsemen we first meet on the grassy downs of Rohan.

However many varieties of Men may exist at the time of the War of the Rings, the central line of Humankind as Tolkien imagines that race dominating the Fourth Age will be mostly (we hope) the descendants of the Nú-menoreans: the Aragorns and Faramirs of the world. But it is true too that in this historical perspective, as in all the others Tolkien has given us, Men are at their best and at their height at the beginning of the Age, and will decline physically and morally as time goes on. Evil will insidiously spread until it must be defeated again, and who can say when that will be? At present we have Faramirs and Aragorns among us, but far too few of them, and are more than generously supplied with Boromirs and Bill Fernys.

Given Tolkien's historical/generic use of the term "Men," this chapter may provide the most logical as well as the most convenient place to speak of his female characters, whatever "race" they may belong to. Many readers have noticed both the scarcity of women in Tolkien's tale, and the rather gingerly way he deals with women characters. Two reasons seem particularly relevant to explain the paucity of women: one is that obviously this is a tale of male-style adventure: of danger, rugged travel, battle, deeds of derring-do; in other words, the kinds of actions that take place typically, or even stereotypically, within a man's world.

The other reason is related to this but is somewhat more culturally bound: one has to call to mind Tolkien's birth in the late nineteenth century and the prevalent standards of the day. There was, for instance, the Victorian notion of "separate spheres" of activity for men and women in the world. Men are out in the world of work, conflict, money, contending in brutal and unforgiving arenas. Women are at home, providing shelter and comfort, supervising the household and the raising of the children—being typically angels of the house. (Oxford University, where Tolkien spent much of his life, enforced this separation of work and home by custom as stringently perhaps as any place in England.)

This separation of responsibilities (dreadfully simple as I have made it here) helps explain why Galadriel can be so noble a figure as a ruler, and also how it is fitting that her task is to preserve the haven of Lothlórien, and always as it were to operate behind the scenes. At a somewhat different location on the social scale and elsewhere in Middle-earth, Rose Cotton is waiting for Sam Gamgee to get back to the Shire and take up the proper business of living.

There are, as noted, remarkably few women in *The Lord of the Rings:* Galadriel, Arwen, Éowyn, Goldberry, Rose Cotton, plus a few who make the merest cameo appearances, such as Farmer Maggot's wife and Frodo's bothersome relative, Lobelia Sackville-Baggins. Elven women may be human women made more perfect, but whether Goldberry, indubitably female, is human, or a nature spirit, or a kind of naiad, or belongs on this list at all, is open to discussion.

It seems clear that Tolkien not only treats his women with an old-fashioned courtliness, or what in Victorian terms might have been called "reverence for womanhood," he also hardly treats them as women at all in any particularized way, except for physical description. Rose Cotton may be waiting at home because that is her role, but her rather limited outlook on world affairs is in her nature as a Hobbit, not in her nature as a female. Hobbits in general are creatures of little imagination, Tolkien has told us, rarely highly educated, and quite Shire-bound in their views. Similarly, the way Galadriel exercises power may be typically womanly, but her possession of that power and her nobility come from her being an Elf, not a female. (Still, it is interesting to see that the Elves' guiding deity or tutelary spirit is herself a female: the Vala called Varda, known to those in exile as Elbereth.)

Of all the women characters, Éowyn of Rohan is the most notable in traditional spheres of action such as war, but she succeeds not by being a woman of Rohan, but by pretending to be a man, or by adopting the masculine values of her warrior nation. She went to war in part, one suspects, because Aragorn rather condescendingly told her to stay home (stay in her "sphere," if you will) and because he could not accept her tendered love. (Unwittingly, Éowyn has been at the center of the only overt mention of human sexuality in the tale: Gríma Wormtongue has long lusted after her, and Saruman has promised Gríma the woman he desired as part of his reward for selling Rohan [see II, 159; *147*].) And there is rather little softness, although there may be true love, in the courtship Éowyn and Faramir undertake while they are confined to the Houses of Healing.

In all, some readers have concluded, Tolkien treats his infrequent women characters respectfully (or in Rose Cotton's case, perhaps, indulgently), but he does not seem vitally interested in them.

Fourteen

Darkness, Evil, and Forms of the Enemy

While the Free Peoples or the forces of Good can be thought of as groups, races, tribes—Ents, Rohirrim, Elves—many of the exemplars of Evil seem to be unique examples, or seem to appear once only. It is not always clear how or to what extent these harmful beings are under Sauron's direct control; some seem to be independently malicious, not working for the Dark Lord but certainly resenting the intrusion of others into their domain. Some forms of evil are not only unconnected with Sauron, but even pre-date his ascendancy, as we shall see.

Frodo and his companions encounter several manifestations of evil in the earliest days of their journey, and when the Fellowship is broken each separate group of travelers encounters its own evil enemies. Given the serial nature of these confrontations, it seems best to talk about each adversary as it crosses the travelers' paths.

Such beings as Orcs or Dark Riders are heard of almost from the beginning of the tale; I have tried to reserve discussion of them here until they actually come face to face with the travelers. But the first kind of foe I need to mention does not appear in this tale at all.

DRAGONS

When Naomi Mitchison queried the existence of dragons in the days of the War of the Rings, Tolkien affirmed that existence. Smaug, after all, had been destroyed only some eighty years earlier, in the days of Bilbo's adventures and the Battle of the Five Armies (in *The Hobbit*). Tolkien wrote that he did not mean to suggest that dragons were extinct at the end of the Third Age. In fact, "they were active in far later times, close to our own."[1]

This remark shows among other things how nicely Tolkien can blend the imaginary (the world of his own creation); the mythical (the world in which St. George and Beowulf and others can war against and defeat the dread Worms); and the historical (the time line of actual years or centuries or eons above which the imaginary and the mythical can hover).

The authority on dragons in Middle-earth itself is of course Gandalf. Speaking of the various Rings, he tells Frodo that the flaming breath of dragons is no longer fierce enough to destroy a Ring of Power (see I, 94; *87*). Thus, not *no* dragons, but no *adequate* dragons.

Dragons may exist somewhere in the land, but they do not, and should not, play any part in this story. By nature self-willed, they certainly would not take service with Sauron; unlike Shelob, they probably would not even co-operate with him. The absence of dragons from *The Lord of the Rings* is appropriate, even if regrettable.

OLD MAN WILLOW

The independent malice spoken of before seems to be the chief attribute of Old Man Willow in the Old Forest. He is one of the earliest obstacles that the Hobbits encounter, and while it is not easy to see the old wretch as a direct agent of Sauron, it is easy to see his hatred.

The Old Forest is a very strange place, says Merry, and in it "'the trees . . . watch you . . . [and they have become] very unfriendly.'" (I, 156–7; *144–5*) And Tom Bombadil, after he has rescued the hobbits from the clutches of Old Man Willow, describes how the trees are resentful of lost power, nursing ancient and not-so-ancient wrongs.

When Merry and Pippin meet Treebeard in Fangorn Forest, they seek to make a connection between his woods and the Old Forest. Treebeard will only concede that both forests still contain stands of black-hearted trees, but he claims that those in Fangorn are "'much worse'" than those off to the north in the Old Forest. (II, 89; *83*) There is some hint in Tom Bombadil's conversation, and a plain implication in Treebeard's, that the evil in the hearts of these trees, in whichever forest, was implanted there when Sauron was openly powerful in Middle-earth. Evil memory remains, as does Sauron's initial responsibility, but the malice seems to be independent here in the latter days of the Third Age.

A conversation between Tom Bombadil and Treebeard on the history and management of forests would be interesting indeed, but we do not have it. Between accounts of the Old Forest, and accounts of Fangorn Forest, there are not so much factual inconsistencies as differences in seriousness of treatment. The full power of a well-led forest is not realized in Tom Bombadil's little land; the power of tree there is directed only against stray individuals.

BARROW-WIGHTS

A couple of days later—it seems hard to keep track of time in Tom Bombadil's country—the party of hobbits encounters the Barrow-wights. The Barrows are the "mounds" covering the "biers of dead kings and queens," as Tom describes them (I, 181; *167*), and the Wights, evil spirits from Angmar who prey upon the dead and upon travelers, are so dreadful that they have been at least heard of as far away as the Shire itself.

The four hobbits escape them, with the help of Tom Bombadil, but the Barrow-wights are part of the wide-flung network of evil that is threatening to cover Middle-earth. For these Wights are indeed from Angmar, the witch-kingdom in the north of Middle-earth beyond the Ettenmoors. The capital of Angmar was Carn Dûm (in the barrow, Merry mutters about Carn Dûm in his dream of evil), and the Witch-King of Angmar is now the Captain of the Nazgûl or Ringwraiths. The evil here is thus not unconnected with other evils the hobbits will meet, but there is also a good result: from the Barrow-downs the weapons of Westernesse will come into the hobbits' hands.

And all this takes place before the hobbits even reach Bree.

THE BLACK RIDERS AND WEATHERTOP

Nine Rings for Mortal Men doomed to die: Sauron presented them to great kings and leaders of Middle-earth, Mortal Men of enormous pride. The Rings enslaved them according to their stature, as Rings of Power do—the prouder the more easily caught—and the nine are now the Nazgûl, or in Westron translation, Ringwraiths, or as they first manifest themselves to the hobbits, Black Riders. These minions of Sauron seem to belong here under a heading of evil forces rather than under a heading of "Men"—Men they once were, but no longer. Just as the One Ring stretches out its bearer's life—so that even Bilbo at the end looks a little thinned out—so the Ringwraiths have become attenuated so that they scarcely exist except as extensions of their master's will. Though the Nazgûl have forms, they are in a peculiar in-between state of life and death.

They are invisible in ordinary light, and they have become so enrapt in a world of shadow and evil that they cannot see under conditions of ordinary light. Yet they have physical bodies—those black robes they wear enclose something—they have voices; yet (again) those bodies are held together by mere acts of will. "Dernhelm" addresses the Captain of the Nazgûl as "'living or dark undead'"—she cannot tell which—and when Merry strikes that blow with his sword from the Barrow-downs, Tolkien tells us that the ancient blade from lost Arnor hews "the undead flesh" (III, 146; *131*) and breaks its bond of spirit. "Undead": like all the other creatures of Sauron, the Ringwraiths, mighty as they once were, have no life or identity of their own. Their captain, the Witch-King, he who fell at the Pelennor Fields, had received his Ring and presumably had become a vassal of Sauron's before ascending the throne of Angmar. He was driven from it about 1975 of the Third Age, and thereafter assembled his eight subordinates at Barad-dûr. He is often called the Lord of the Nazgûl.

Frodo and Sam have seen the army he leads issuing forth from Minas Morgul a few days before the Battle of the Pelennor Fields, but when he falls, another, called Gothmog, gives orders in his stead and throws fresh troops into the fray. Is this a Nazgûl? Or is this entity like the Mouth of Sauron at the Morannon a living man, a Black Númenorean? Within the context of the story, we cannot tell.[2]

Only Frodo has actually ever seen a Nazgûl, in the encounter at Weathertop mentioned in Chapter 3 above. There are five on the hilltop and when Frodo, unable to resist, puts on the Ring, he can see them "terribly" clearly. (I, 263; *240*) Their hands are haggard, their hairs are gray, their faces white. (They are a little reminiscent of the "pale kings and princes" whom Keats's knight sees enthralled in "La Belle Dame Sans Merci.") They are terrible, and merciless, and evil, but they are also old and drawn out to a fine point. Having lost all will they do not recognize their slavery. They have tremendous power—they can terrify with their screams and their exudations—but they also have limitations. They must, for instance, move about as ordinary men do, on horseback or, later, on the backs of nameless winged creatures (doubtless these creatures are parodies of the great eagles who rescue and carry Gandalf and others at crucial moments). They suffer these physical limitations since they are in basic ways physical beings but they also, like their master, suffer that lack of imagination which augurs well for the Free.

CREBAIN

After the Company of Nine is formed and leaves Rivendell, four manifestations of evil occur before they reach the Doors of Moria. Each seems singular or unique; the role of Sauron in each cannot be certainly stated; none happens again. But a plausible case can be made that these are orchestrated events, not random happenings or whimsical inventions of Tolkien's. They *can* be explained as part of a strategy concerted by Sauron and Saruman to defeat Frodo's mission, and specifically to defeat it by attempting to destroy Gandalf. We learn a little later that both Sauron and Saruman have Seeing Stones and are in communication. Saruman doubtless believes that the *palantíri* are allowing two grand wizardly spirits to confer on equal terms, and it is likely that Sauron is content to let him believe that.

As the Company passes southward through Hollin, one of the many empty lands they traverse, Sam, standing watch one day, sees a flock of crow-like birds flying low overhead. Aragorn tells Gandalf that these are "'*cre-bain* . . . spying out the land.'" (I, 371–3; *340–1*) Crows are birds of dark menace in most traditional contexts, but whose birds are these? The apparent answer is that they are Saruman's; when Aragorn and the others meet Éomer on the plains of Rohan many weeks later, he tells them that Saruman has sent forth "'birds of ill omen.'" (II, 48; *46*) Considering that Sam and Aragorn first spotted the *crebain* coming from the south, that is, from the direction of Isengard, this identification of their sender is not at all improbable. A bird was the means of Gandalf's escape from Orthanc, and it would not be surprising if Saruman has his own avian agents on the watch for the wizard, even though more than three months have passed.

MOUNT CARADHAS

The next assault on the party comes as they attempt to cross Mount Carad-has by way of the Redhorn Pass—their optimal route over the Misty Mountains. But Caradhas foils them with intense but highly localized snow. It is not clear that this bad weather has anything to do with Sauron or his minions, even though it helps them; it may simply be the ill-nature of nature, for, as Aragorn observes, many evil forces are out there, quite independent of Sauron (see I, 378; *346*).

Certainly this is true, but as Gandalf in his turn asserts, the arm of the Enemy has grown long, and he may be capable of such contrivances as this. The immediate effect of the storm is to reveal Gandalf as he works a spell to light a fire—by the great spout of green and blue flame it produces. Anyone for hundreds of miles around could see the unique signature of Gandalf's work. The ultimate effect of the storm is to drive the party to take the most dangerous way possible past the mountain barrier—beneath it, through the Mines of Moria, a route fraught with peril especially and specifically for Gandalf, as Aragorn warns him.

WARGS

Wargs appear in *The Hobbit* as the fiercest of wolves: wolves of some intelligence who chase Bilbo and his dwarf friends into the treetops. Gandalf drives them off with bolts of vivid fire, for wolves "are afraid of fire." Finally the wolves flee "yammering and looking for water."[3]

But the Wargs the Company encounters the night after the retreat from Caradhas are far from their usual hunting grounds. They have come west of the mountains, Aragorn exclaims as the wolves encircle the Nine in darkness. "'Hound of Sauron!'" Gandalf calls the leader of the pack; Legolas fells one with his bow and arrow, and the pack withdraws. The wolves return and the Company engages them fully, but in the light of morning there are no wolves to be found, even though many had been slain. (I, 389–91; *355–7*)

"'These were no ordinary wolves,'" says Gandalf, and that seems to be a bit of an understatement. He is the only one (to our knowledge) who has met Wargs before (in the *Hobbit* incident just mentioned). He had to use fire then, and he has to use fire now, repeating the incantation with which he produced flame on the mountain-path, and adding, "'*Naur dan i ngaurhoth!*'"[4]

These were spectral wolves—*were*-wolves in the most literal sense. Were they a sending of Sauron's? The most important thing about the incident may be the drain on Gandalf's strength, for he is exhausted when he has to face the Balrog some time later.

THE WATCHER

As the party nears the west Gate of Moria, they find that the Gate-stream, the Sirannon, which Gandalf remembers as a brisk-flowing brook has become a mere trickle. It has been dammed up to form a shallow lake with an outflowing stream of filthy water across which the Company must wade, much to their disgust.

As they are about to enter the Doors of Moria, something in the shallow lake or pool, an arm or tentacle, grabs Frodo and starts dragging him toward the water. Sam rescues Frodo, but the creature—octopus or kraken or whatever it may be—seizes the open doors and smashes them shut so that even Gandalf cannot open them again. Later in the Chamber of Records, the Company learns that the Watcher has been at the Gate at least since Balin and his Dwarves returned to Moria: it took the Dwarf Óin. Gandalf also notes that this time the thing grabbed the Ring-bearer; unstated but equally plain is the fact that it has shut the entire group, including Gandalf himself, inside the mountain to face whatever may be there.

Thus it can be argued that everything that happens between Rivendell and Moria is directed at Gandalf as much as at anyone: the crows spy him out, the storm forces him toward Moria, the fire forces him both to reveal himself and to expend some of his strength in magic, the Wargs make him spend more, and the Watcher in the waters cuts off any retreat westward once the group has fled into the Mines.

Everything has driven Gandalf toward his confrontation with the Balrog, and in that confrontation Gandalf falls. The loss of Gandalf is an evil and terrible thing, not only for the Company, and Frodo himself, but for the entire cause of the Free Peoples. Yet, in accordance with Tolkien's moral arithmetic, evil intent yields (eventually) good result: Gandalf falls, yes, but he returns strengthened and empowered, as Gandalf the White—made more fit to lead the West against the Dark Lord.

ORCS

We have heard of Orcs many times before Frodo's journey began and during its earlier stages, but not until they are in the Mines of Moria does the Company actually face them and have to fight them. The *word* "orc," Tolkien tells us, derives from Old English for "demon,"[5] and the creatures themselves are ancient in Middle-earth.

Orcs are called goblins in *The Hobbit*: it is a less grown-up name for these spawns of darkness. They are bow-legged, long-armed, fanged, squat but muscular, hairy, and they smell bad. Within these general descriptive limits there are some interesting variations among orcs.

Treebeard the Ent speaks somewhat amiss when he says that Orcs were made as "counterfeits" of Elves in the olden days (as trolls were of Ents). (II,

113; *105*) To counterfeit something is to make it as like the original as possible, so as to fool whoever encounters it. Black and red $100 bills with portraits of Benedict Arnold would not answer the need at all.

Treebeard's error is understandable: he is, as Tolkien told an inquirer, a character in the story, with a character's necessarily limited knowledge, and he is not in any case one of the wise, despite having a fund of practical wisdom and a long memory.[6] Given the disparity in the appearances of Orcs and Elves, and even of trolls and Ents, Treebeard seems to mean something more like "parody," and indeed he goes on to use the word "mockery" to describe the achievement (if not the intention) of this act of production. The notion of parody is carried out in some detail: the Elves, for instance, have a delicious restorative drink called *miruvor,* with which Gandalf doses his companions from time to time. The Orcs have a foul-tasting Orc draught that Merry and Pippin find has a similar if cruder effect.

Frodo speaks more accurately than Treebeard when he tells Sam that the Enemy did not bring these creatures into being in an originational sense at all; speaking of Orcs' physical needs, Frodo says that they have to have food and water: "'The Shadow that bred them can only mock, it cannot make . . . it only ruined [orcs and] they have to live like other living creatures.'" (III, 233; *210*)

Frodo's viewpoint is also sounder than Treebeard's considered as traditional theology: Evil as mere negation must be profoundly uncreative. The viewpoint is also more consistent with what we are told in *The Silmarillion:* that those of the Elves "who came into the hands of Melkor . . . were corrupted and enslaved; and thus did Melkor breed . . . Orcs in envy and mockery of Elves. . . ."[7] So even Sauron's great master, Melkor, could only ruin and twist creatures already alive.

In *The Lord of the Rings* we meet several kinds of Orcs, as we meet several kinds of Elves. The first kind belong to Sauron and probably constitute the bulk of the fighting Orcs we see in the tale. They are "large and evil: black Uruks of Mordor" (I, 421; *384*), whom Gandalf and the others meet in Moria. But later, when Merry and Pippin are force-marched across the fields of Rohan, the reprehensible Uglúk boasts, "'We are the fighting Uruk-hai! We slew [Boromir].'" (II, 61; *58*) In the conversation in which Uglúk makes his brag, his is the "growling" voice; a softer "but more evil" voice belongs to Grishnákh, who says Orcs and prisoners alike should go back to Lugbúrz (Mordor, apparently, or perhaps the Dark Tower itself) and demands, "'Who does Saruman think he is?'" There is a third group, Northern Orcs, the ones who cannot stand daylight (these Tolkien does call "goblins," maybe to suggest that they are not of much account). At all events, the three factions quarrel constantly as they race across the Wold of Rohan, until they finally meet the Men of Rohan and are destroyed, and Merry and Pippin escape.

The quarrels of the Orcs reflect the enmity of their masters, Sauron and Saruman. If Saruman has the stronger and bigger Orcs, Sauron has the more sinister ones—they are driven by a will far more powerful than the wizard's. The point has already been made but may be worth repeating: the evil of the Orcs makes them untrusting and untrustworthy. In each case—here on the plains of Rohan with Merry and Pippin, later in the Tower of Cirith Ungol with Frodo and Sam and the almost comically vulgar Shagrat and Gorbag, and later still with Frodo and Sam on the march across Mordor—their evil intent leads to good result for the Hobbits. In all three cases the result is escape.

And not only do these internal quarrels aid the Hobbits; they also harm the Orcs themselves. Arguments which come to knife-point can only impede decision, and action, and military movement. Blame-laying is also a favorite diversion of these Orcs: their worms'-eye view of what is going on among top strategists gives us a refreshingly irreverent perspective on supposedly terrible and powerful Evil.

Treebeard, by the way, may not be completely astray when he suggests that Saruman may have cross-bred Orcs and Men to produce the powerful Uruk-hai (see II, 96; *90*). If Orcs were only twisted and corrupted Elves in the beginning, and if Men and Elves can produce offspring (as they have), then the thing is not unthinkable, although you would not want to picture it. The squint-eyed southerner at Bree may be such a half-breed, as may some of the "large ill-favoured Men" the hobbits find at *The Green Dragon* when they finally return to the Shire. These Men remind Sam of the southerner, in fact, and Merry says he is reminded of soldiers he saw at Isengard.

Tolkien's genetic rules can be pretty flexible, after all.

THE BALROG

Several species or "races" survive from the First Age of Middle-earth into the Third: Elves, Dwarves, and Men, to name only the most obvious. Very few individuals, however, have survived over those thousands of years: the High Elves, certainly. Probably not Gandalf—not in Middle-earth anyway: he did not come into Middle-earth until about the year 1000 of the Third Age; although he spent a long youth in the West as Olórin. Tom Bombadil and Treebeard might be added to this short list.

Among the powers of evil, Melkor or Morgoth's corrupted Elves, the Orcs, survive. Sauron himself, the Maia who was Morgoth's chief lieutenant, has survived, and so, it turns out, has at least one of the race of fire demons or Balrogs, Maiar who followed Morgoth into darkness, lying in the depths of Middle-earth. The Balrog seems to have slumbered beneath Moria until the Dwarves dug too avariciously for the precious metal *mithril* "'and disturbed that from which they fled, Durin's Bane,'" says Gandalf. (I, 413; *377–8*) That was in Third Age 1980; Balin and his group re-entered Moria in 2989, and presumably met a similar fate: Ori's scrawl in the Book of Mazarbul speaks of drums, just like the drums his readers are now hearing. Now, as then, the Orcs approach—and so does something else.

There is no doubt that the "something" that Gandalf describes as "dark as a cloud" in the Chamber of Records, and laying a terrible counterspell on its door (I, 425; *388*), something of which even the Orcs are afraid, something about which they kept saying "ghâsh" or "fire," is the Balrog. Only Gandalf and Legolas, of that Company, recognize it: "'A Balrog!'" Legolas cries, naming its kind. (I, 428; *391*)

Tall, or rather huge, winged, dark or flame-wrapped, wielding a whip, mute, and terrible in its very silence, the Balrog embodies all that one would wish to see of Hell. If there can be majesty in evil, the Balrog possesses it. "'[F]lame of Udûn!'" Gandalf challenges it, calling himself "'wielder of the flame of Anor'" (I, 429; *392*), that is, the Sun, the clear light of day, purifying flame, good. (Udûn is a word with several possible meanings; in the context, "hell" would do admirably.) In the titanic confrontation that ensues, Gandalf eventually destroys the flame-shrouded monster.

There "is usually a hang-over especially of evil from one age to another," Tolkien said,[8] and if there can be a consolation for all the losses of excellence and variety that the end of the Third Age brings, it may be that some terrible evils will also disappear.

SHELOB

Shelob, the giant spider that lurks in the Pass of Cirth Ungol, is severely injured, but it is not clear that she disappears as the War of the Rings and the Third Age draw to a close. Sam wounds her and blinds her: she may, as Robert Foster suggests, die of her wounds or die of starvation because in her blindness she cannot hunt.[9]

Shelob is unusual in that among all the allies of Sauron, she is the most independent. Other creatures of Sauron, such as the trolls we see at the Morannon, or even the Nazgûl themselves, are driven and energized by his will. When that will wavers or is withdrawn, they waver and collapse. But Shelob in her foul mountain lair serves Sauron's interests only as long as he fulfills hers, which are for food, or for the essence of life itself. (She mates with her own offspring, and is no doubt responsible for the broods of spiders in Mirkwood which caused Bilbo and his companions so much trouble in *The Hobbit*.)

Much has been said about Shelob in Chapter 7 and need not be repeated here. Just as "no tale tells" what happened to her ancestor Ungoliant in the First Age, except that Ungoliant may have fled southward from the regions controlled by Morgoth and afterward perished,[10] so "no tale tells" (the very formula) how Shelob came to Cirith Ungol. (II, 422; *393*)

Shelob is probably the most horrific single entity that Frodo and Sam must face on their journey to the Fiery Mountain.

THE TWO WATCHERS

But Sam must also deal with the Two Watchers: three-headed, vulturine, semi-sentient guardians who cast an invisible beam or barrier across the gateway of the Tower of Cirith Ungol, a kind of force field, but one that has physical power rather than the psychological power of terror the Nazgûl possess.

These multi-headed figures on guard are reminiscent of Cerberus, the three-headed dog which guarded the entrance to Hades. They are stone statues, although they have glittering eyes and strong wills; yet like most things in the land of Sauron, who cannot tolerate rival life, they are barely above the level of mineral existence. Their wills, like the wills of the Nazgûl and others of Sauron's creatures, are but a tiny corner of his own dark will.

And just as the Nazgûl can be cowed or rendered ineffective by language, and Shelob by language and light, so these Watchers: Sam breaks their will momentarily by showing the Phial of Galadriel, and gains entrance to the Tower; on the way out he and Frodo show the Phial again, and cry out in Elvish. The power of the Watchers is instantly shattered (see III, 235; *212*) and the two hobbits escape by a hairsbreadth.

TROLLS AND HILL-TROLLS

Generally, trolls are comically stupid creatures, as Bilbo found in *The Hobbit*, and as Sam reminds us when he recites his poem at the lair of Bilbo's petrified victims. But it would seem that the Dark Lord has been at work (another breeding program evidently) and has brought into action a race of extraordinarily powerful and malevolent trolls. We see trolls aiding the Balrog: they are bringing up great stone slabs to bridge the fiery fissure across the Second Hall of Old Moria (I, 428; *391*); we see them at the Gates of Minas Tirith, where they are wielding Grond, the great ram which will break those gates. (III, 125; *112*) And at the battle before the Black Gate of Morannon, the last stand of the Free Peoples, taken even as Frodo reaches the Cracks of Doom, there come fearsome "hill-trolls out of Gorgoroth. . . . Like a storm they broke upon the line of the men of Gondor. . . ." (III, 207; *187*) Even as Pippin watches, one of them fells the faithful guard Beregond, but in his last conscious act on that field, Pippin stabs upward with his own sword of Westernesse and slays the creature.

There is nothing comic about these hill-trolls: they are a real menace in battle, and they are also a psychological weapon which Sauron has brought out, calculated to dismay Gandalf's puny forces. But they too are actuated only by Sauron's will, and when his will is removed at the moment the Ring of Power is destroyed, trolls and gates and towers all alike fall.

Fifteen

ON LANGUAGES

Tolkien's love of languages as the bedrock foundation for his story has been mentioned often. If one word—"Mellon" or "Friend"—can open the Doors of Moria, language itself is the passkey to the world of Middle-earth. So much detailed and recondite scholarship exists on Tolkien's professional knowledge of real-world languages and literatures, his use of them in building his Middle-earth languages, and the deployment and familial relationships of languages within Middle-earth, that this chapter can attempt nothing new. It is written by a non-specialist for non-specialists, and tries to deal with inevitable questions in as non-technical a way as possible.[1]

THE TONGUES OF MIDDLE-EARTH

Schematically the language question is less complex than it may appear. Complications arise in questions of linguistic survivals in place-names and personal names, in mixed forms, and so on. For Tolkien has, even though his languages are his personal creation, given them a history: like languages in our world, they have changed over time, word-forms have become worn down (sometimes almost to the point of unrecognizability), word-forms are mixed in origin, languages borrow words from one another, peoples adopt their own versions of other peoples' languages. Most of the features of linguistic history that European languages show are replicated in the languages of Middle-earth.

Likewise, the languages reflect the political fortunes of the races or groups that speak them. Likewise also, languages reflect social status: it is often enough the case that the rulers of a given realm (say, Lothlórien) will speak or be able to speak a different language from that of its ordinary inhabitants.

To repeat, the language matter is less complicated than it may seem, because although a number of languages are mentioned (and discussed thoroughly in the Appendices), and each ethnic group or "race" has its language, and each language is related to others in Middle-earth in systematic ways, the actual representations of alien languages or invented languages are rather slight. The two varieties of Elvish described below do present enough material to enable scholars to construct grammars, but their vocabularies are fairly limited. Other languages exist either in the form of a group of proper nouns, or largely in fragments: a battle cry in Dwarvish, the two lines of the inscription on the Ring in the Black Speech of Mordor.

Elven languages reflect the events of their ancient history. There were East-Elves who totally ignored the Summons to the West, and there were West-Elves, subdivided into Elves who actually made the journey over Sea in response to the Summons (see Chapter 10 above), or those who started on the Great Journey but lingered in the western coastlands of Middle-earth. Those who went and returned in exile were High-Elves or *Eldar.* They spoke a language called *Quenya,* which has become what Tolkien calls "Elven-Latin," the language they use only for solemn and formal occasions. (III, 506; *468*) Tolkien wrote that *Quenya* could be thought of as based in Latin, with materials from two other languages whose sounds and structure he enjoyed: Finnish and Greek.[2] For everyday use, the Elves adopted, upon their return to Middle-earth, the Elven language of those who had stayed, which was *Sindarin* or Grey-Elven. *Sindarin,* Tolkien tells us, was constructed out of his love of Welsh, and was designed to resemble that Celtic tongue.[3]

Elven conversations with non-Elvish speakers are conducted in the Common Speech, rendered as English, thus most of the examples of actual Elven we have occur in songs and poems. But all the Elves we meet, Elrond, Legolas, Glorfindel, and others would be speaking Sindarin in appropriate contexts as an everyday matter. The examples of Elvish we do have vary.

Although Hobbits are notoriously uninterested in abstruse subjects like linguistics, Frodo and Bilbo are both distinguished among them for knowing some Elvish. Frodo can recognize High-Elvish speech, as he recognizes Gildor and his band as High-Elven because they speak of Elbereth, and he can even utter a few phrases in the High-Elven tongue; back in the Shire when he greeted Gildor, the Elf laughingly called Frodo a scholar (see I, 119; *120*). Ruth Noel tells us that the lovely song which Frodo hears at Rivendell, "A Elbereth Gilthoniel" (I, 312; *286*), is in *Sindarin,* while the "Farewell to Lórien" or "Galadriel's Lament," sung by her, is in the ancient *Quenya,*[4] and Tolkien notes that "Frodo did not understand the words." (I, 489; *445*) So it appears that Frodo's scholarship in Elvish is laudable but his knowledge of the "Ancient Tongue" is confined to a few formulaic expressions, like greetings.

These two uses of the two varieties of Elvish are, however, entirely appropriate: Sindarin in Rivendell, a place where there is memory of ancient things, and where people from many lands meet and mix, Quenya in Lothlórien, a hidden realm where ancient things still live on. (Use of Quenya even in the Golden Wood is quite limited, however; the common coin of language is Sindarin.) In sum, then, Quenya is the Elvish language form used in ceremony, ritual, and art song. Sindarin is the Elvish language form used in the conduct of ordinary life, including communal singing. (Other Elvish languages such as those of the East-Elves are not heard in the story.)

The languages of Men (human beings) are if anything more complicated, and their passage down the years follows a diverse pattern—as diverse as the groups of Men who speak them. The various sub-classes here include (1) Men who were associated with Númenor and the West, and thus in one way or another with Elves, and whose languages are so marked; (2) Men of Middle-earth who have been in some way associated with the first sub-class (such as the Rohirrim); (3) Men belonging to linguistic populations that have always been relatively isolated (the Woses, for instance); and (4) Hobbits, who, whatever their feelings on the question, have to be considered under the heading of Men for discussion of language.

First, Númenoreans, Men of Westernesse, the Dunédain, had a native language, their ancestral Mannish tongue called Adûnaic. But in the high days of Númenor they also knew and used the Elvish Sindarin and learned it through successive generations, as English speakers might know French or Spanish. The more learned among the Númenoreans also knew and reverenced Quenya (as we might learn and admire Latin). One sign of growing folly and pride in Númenor was the abandonment of this Elvish learning.

But the loyal Númenoreans who came to Middle-earth after the downfall of the kingdom at the end of the Second Age retained some of their linguistic skill. They used the Common Speech of the Middle-earth folk among whom they dwelt but enriched it with many Elven borrowings. This heightened speech was the common currency of Gondor, and it seems to have existed alongside actual Elvish. When Frodo and Sam are taken in Ithilien, two of Faramir's men, Mablung and Damrod, are assigned to guard them. The two men talk together, speaking first in the Common Speech "and then changing to a language of their own." Listening, Frodo is astonished to find that they are speaking some variant of Elvish, and so he knows that these are descendants, however distant, of the Men of Númenor.

In the northward regions, Men spoke an Adûnaic related to the language of Númenor and a language somewhat like the Common Speech. These are the languages of, say, Western Mirkwood and of Dale.

Second, from this northern region came (lately, in terms of Middle-earth history) the Rohirrim, who settled in what is now Rohan. They kept their ancestral language (which Tolkien has drawn to resemble Old English or Anglo-Saxon) but also, being allies of Gondor, spoke that ennobled version of the Common Speech or Westron spoken in Minas Tirith. All the items of Rohirric vocabulary are drawn from Old English: Ruth Noel lists 98 items, mostly proper names.[5]

Third, alien or unrelated tongues include the language of the Woses of the Stonewain Valley, whose broken version of "English" or the Common

Speech is more a result of rustiness than of primitiveness. They wish only to be left alone, and to have only minimal interchange with the rest of Middle-earth.

Here discussion of the tongues of Men brings us to a country, a people, and a language otherwise scarcely mentioned in *The Lord of the Rings:* Dunland, and the Dunlendings and their tongue. Both the Men of Bree (of whom more below) and these Dunlendings are said to be descendants, by blood and by language, of the Dead Men of Dunharrow (those men, that is, whose spirits were released after Aragorn rode the Paths of the Dead and bade them fulfill their oaths). On the maps Dunland can be seen northwest of Rohan and just south of Moria, where the Company passed under the Misty Mountains. The Dunlendings are inveterate enemies of Rohan, whose blond men and women they derisively call "Strawheads," or "Forgoil," the only word of their language we know. (III, 509; *470*) They join the Orcs against Rohan at Helm's Deep; many enemies are shouting "'in the Dunland tongue,'" says Gamling the Old there, a language once widely used in Rohan. He goes on to explain that the Dunlendings still resent after centuries the coming of the Rohirrim and that Saruman has inflamed that resentment to hatred. (II, 180; *167*) None of this rich background in Dunland language is at all necessary to mere plot, which is a token of how fundamental Tolkien's love of language is.

The Men of Bree were said to be of the same ancient origin as the Dunlendings; indeed they claimed to be Bree's "original inhabitants." (I, 205; *188*) Unlike their remote cousins of Dunland, the Men of Bree had been in place for long ages, and, being friendlier than Men usually are with Hobbits, Dwarves, and others, had long since adopted the Westron language as their own.

Fourth, the Hobbits, as Tolkien's whole tale shows, are a highly adaptable people. They have no native language of record. Their former tongue, from before their settlement in Eriador, in what is now the Shire, was like that of Rohan, or, among the Stoors, some tongue akin to Dunlendish. A few old words like "mathom" (for useless things that cannot be thrown away) and some personal names survive from the older times; they are in fact traceable to Rohirric (Old English) or have cognates there.

Assuming his familiar pose as a translator of records of Middle-earth, Tolkien gives some hints in Appendix F of that difficult art, especially as it relates to the Hobbits. For the Common Speech, or Westron, is only *represented* as English in the tale. A place like Elrond's Last Homely House East of the Sea could be called "Imladris" (Elvish) or "Rivendell" (the Englishing of its Westron name, which was *Karningul*). Places like the Shire had to be called "the Shire": to use, or also use, its name in Westron, "Suza," would create a misleadingly alien sense of the place. Names which were totally familiar or usual to the Hobbits (whose point of view is important throughout the tale) had to be presented as names totally usual for English-speaking readers.

In a sense then, Westron is another complete language of Tolkien's invention, but one that he had to conceal thoroughly in order to tell his story. The net effect of Tolkien's discussion of Hobbit language, or Hobbit linguistic usage, is thus to give the studious reader an odd sense of what Westron or the Common Speech of Middle-earth is "really" like. The Shire is "Suza," names like "Sam" and "Ham" for the Gamgee males are "really" Ban and Ran, which in turn are shortenings of *Banazîr* and *Ranugad*. To parallel this archaic Shire usage, "Sam" and "Ham" are shortenings of "Samwise" and "Hamfast," which in turn are updatings of Old "English *samwís* and *hamfæst,*" which mean "half-wise" and "home-fast" or "stay at home." (III, 517; *478*) All this is perhaps more a good demonstration of Tolkien's thoroughness in working through his language patterns for Middle-earth than it is valuable for the average reader.

The matter of translation can lead to difficulties of its own, however. In the Mines of Moria Gandalf and the others come upon the tomb of Balin, on which an inscription is written in the old character system called Daeron's Runes, in, as Gandalf says, "'the tongues of Men and of Dwarves:

BALIN SON OF FUNDIN
LORD OF MORIA'" (I, 416; *380*)

Working out the bottom line of runes, we find that it says phonetically *in English*, "Balin son of Fundin Lord of Moria." We must assume that the translator has given us not the actual runes on the stone (which would be in

Westron, the "tongue of Men"), but the runic English equivalent: again Westron must be concealed for reader ease.

Men and Elves comprise some of the more significant language groups in Middle-earth at the end of the Third Age, but several other languages are represented in the tale. The specimens we have of these languages are brief and fragmentary, which is not to suggest that their speakers are in any way unimportant.

Entish, for example, is a tongue that by its very character would require volumes for adequate representation. It is an "unhasty" language, as Pippin thinks to himself at the Entmoot, where the Ents "murmur slowly," then begin to chant monotonously. (II, 106; *99*)

In Entish every word is a narrative. Treebeard has told the Hobbits that in his language names tell you the history of what they designate and "'it takes a very long time to say anything. . . .'" A moment later he gives an example, calling the little knoll or high spot on which they are standing "'this *a-lalla-lalla-rumba-kamanda-lind-or-burúmë*.'" A moment after that he calls "'these Orcs'" "'these *burárum*.'" (II, 86; *80–1*)[6]

Tolkien characterizes the Ents' speech as unique: "slow . . . repetitive, indeed long-winded," and reminds us in his pose as historian and translator that he is only relaying what the young hobbits (scatter-brained as they are) thought they heard Treebeard saying. It is "probably very inaccurate" (III, 510; *472*) as a rendering of real Entish, he notes.

Equally fragmentary is what we can read of Dwarvish, or Khuzdul, the speech that Aulë devised for his Dwarves when he fashioned them (see Chapter 12). Except for place-names already mentioned like Khazad-dûm for Moria, we have of Gimli's tongue only his war-cry at Helm's Deep, "'*Baruk Khazâd! Khazâd ai-mênu!*'" (II, 177, 178; *164, 165*), that is, "Axes of the Dwarves! The Dwarves are upon you!" and the word "mazarbul," which means "records" or "documents," as Gimli says in Moria (I, 419; *382*) when the Company examines the blackened and burnt pages of the Book of Mazarbul.[7] It is a language strong in "jagged" consonants like "z" and "k" and sparing in open vowels like "e": a sturdy stony language like the people who speak it.

Faintly similar to the Dwarves' language in their outward harsh appearance, but of course nothing like it in character or origin, are the Black Speech of Mordor and the Orkish tongue(s) presumably derived from it. The Black Speech is electrifyingly evil: when Gandalf at the Council of Elrond reads:

> *"Ash nazg durbatulûk, ash nazg gimbatul, ash nazg*
> *thrakatulûk agh burzum-ishi krimpatul!"*

the words sound "menacing, powerful, harsh. . . . the Elves stopped their ears." (I, 333; *305*) (As Elvish is hurtful to the ears of the servants of Sauron—as Frodo showed on Weathertop—so is the Black Speech hurtful to the ears of the good.) When Elrond chides Gandalf for daring to speak in that tongue in this place, Gandalf replies that it will be heard throughout Middle-earth unless the Council acts.

The brief passage in the Black Speech tells us a great deal about the importance of languages in *The Lord of the Rings.* Their importance lies not just in Tolkien's inventiveness, or his ability to invest his made languages with beauty or horror, but equally in the uses to which he puts them.

On the Ring, the language of Mordor has become a symbol of both power and evil. It is meant to be perceived as a language of surpassing ugliness, and its ugliness is just the audible equivalent of its evil. Harsh menace is in its very tones, and hearing it becomes a way of understanding, as Gandalf implies, how dreadful Middle-earth will be under the dominion of its chief speaker.

The moral quality of the languages of Middle-earth is one of their benchmarks. But they are not just tokens: if you are going to have beautiful languages (as Tolkien meant Elvish, for instance, to be to English-accustomed ears) and ugly languages, in a language-centered world, then you have language as part of the very structure of that world.

So language exhibits the moral structure of the world in which it is used. It serves as a form of moral notation for qualities such as evil, or good. Equally important, as you would expect in a work of fictional art, it exhibits the characters of individuals who talk. Since we never hear Sauron speak, except in the minds of other individuals, this use is better shown in the mouths of his lowly servants, the Orcs of Mordor who drive Merry and Pippin across Rohan. One Orc reviles the Orcs of Saruman, then trails off into his own tongue: "'Curse the Isengarders! *Uglúk u bagronk sha push-dug Saruman-glob búbhosh skai.*'" (II, 59; *56*) The prevalence of "hard" sounds like b's and k's and g's, grating sounds like "sh," the absence of "smooth" vowels (notably present in Elvish) represents Tolkien's attempt to create what he has called a "hideous" language. For lack of context and vocabulary the Orc's words are untranslatable, but their general intent can easily be inferred. (The general resemblance to the Black Speech can also be seen: Orkish may be an imitation of the Master's language, or a degenerate dialect of it.)

By contrast, and not very far away, Legolas Greenleaf is hearing the speech of the Men of Rohan for the first time. He appraises Rohan and its people by their language as Aragorn chants a poem in it. He says that the language "'is like to this land itself; rich and rolling in part, and else hard and stern as the mountains. . . . it is laden with the sadness of Mortal Men.'" (II, 142; *132*) As Legolas and his companions approach the hall of King Théoden they are challenged in that same language and Gandalf asks why the guard doesn't use the Common Tongue, which is understood everywhere in the West. One of the guards replies that Théoden has forbidden any to come in except "'those who know our tongue and are our friends.'" (II, 143; *133*) There is something faintly naïve about the conviction that knowledge of one's language premises friendship, but a kind of defiant parochialism is a hallmark of the culture of Rohan.

What Tolkien is pointing out, both within and beyond the borders of Rohan, is the false notion that monolingualism is a virtue. Indeed in a world where most operations of commerce and everyday life in general require at least two languages (one's own and the Common Speech), to speak only one language is to be at a distinct disadvantage. It both suggests and creates isolationism: for instance, the voluntary self-satisfied isolation of most Hobbits, who follow Gaffer Gamgee in believing that they are "queer folk" off there in Buckland (I, 105; *97*), which is all of forty miles away. In knowing a little Elvish, Frodo and Bilbo are not only distinguished but also peculiar.

Similarly, in a protected enclave like Lothlórien, monolingualism suggests the kind of isolation imposed by security measures or by a sense of fear. The Elf Haldir tells Frodo at the borders of the Golden Wood that he and his fellows rarely speak any language except their own, and shun outsiders (see I, 444; *405*). At the moment, Haldir is speaking the Common Speech, but haltingly and, we can sense, reluctantly. Thus, in a way, the language one doesn't use in Middle-earth has as much significance as the language one does use.

So not just language but linguistic competence becomes an index of attitudes (complacent Hobbits, suspicious Elves, hostile Men of Rohan). And in at least one amusing incident, pretension to linguistic knowledge reveals emptiness of mind: when in the Houses of Healing Aragorn calls for *athelas,* or in the language of country-folk, *kingsfoil,* the herb-master proudly demonstrates that he knows the name of the plant in several languages, but adds that they keep none of it in their dispensary. Gandalf cries, "'go and find some old man of less lore and more wisdom who keeps some in his house!'" (III, 172; *155*) Clearly, knowing the substance and value of a thing implies knowing its name or several of them; the herb-master's pedantry suggests that the reverse is not necessarily true.

THE WRITING SYSTEMS OF MIDDLE-EARTH

Who can read? The societies of Middle-earth are by and large literate societies in all their many languages. But inquiry into details of literacy brings oddly mixed results. Most Orcs, for instance, would not be thought of as lettered, but Tolkien tells us that the writing called runes was known "even to orcs." (III, 493; *455*) The Wild Men of the Stonewain Valley are intelligent folk but probably have no written records, nor do the Ents. The Men of Rohan lay claim to a mostly oral tradition but the epitaph on the stone at Snowmane's Howe (the burial mound of Théoden's unfortunate horse) is written in the languages of Gondor and Rohan (see III, 146; *131–2*). And Hobbits of course have their own priorities in life skills: they all can cook, Tolkien tells us, but many cannot read or write (see II, 330; *308*).

What inhabitants of Middle-earth read, if they can read, comes in two forms, or two systems of characters, with variants and a developmental history for each. You can tell from Tolkien's discussion of them that he took both great delight and great pains in devising them. He was a scrupulously exact penman, and labored hard at his calligraphic efforts, as the creation of the damaged pages from the Book of Mazarbul would suggest. A 1947 letter to Katherine Farrer is in runes, another to Hugh Brogan in 1948 employs runes and both variants of the *Tengwar*.[8] His own signature bears some resemblance to that script.

First there was a set of angular linear figures analogous to our "runes," meant originally to be carved or incised, or scratched, and called the *Certar* or *Cirth*. In its most highly developed form this set of characters was called "Daeron's Runes," after its deviser, Daeron, a minstrel of Doriath in early times. It was adopted, modified somewhat, and widely used by the Dwarves as well as others. The Dwarves called these runes *Angerthas Moria,* or the Long Rune-rows of Moria. Tolkien sets them out in the tables at III, 502–3; *464–5,* and they can be seen in the inscription on Balin's tomb in Moria.

Closer to what we think of as letters, in their cursive characters with loops and strokes, are the *Tengwar,* devised by Fëanor (the same Elven genius who may have fashioned the *palantíri*) and arranged in a logical tabular classification of sound values (see III, 494; *456,* and Tolkien's annotations on the meanings of the symbols). One system of the *Tengwar* represents vowel sounds by superscript strokes or marks (usually called *tehtar*), while another represents the vowels with separate characters of their own (see III, 498; *460*). This is how the inscription on the West Door of Moria is shown (see I, 398–9; *364–5*).

The writing on the title pages of the three parts of *The Lord of the Rings* is in these character sets, but the language is English, and is not meant to represent the full range of graphic possibilities. Thus the only writings we have that are in both the languages and written characters of Middle-earth are:

- the inscription on the One Ring, represented as written in "an ancient mode" of Elvish script, but in the language of the Ring-maker, Sauron, the Black Speech: it is shown at I, 80; *75,* given in English at I, 81; *75,* and presented in its original language but in the Roman alphabet at I, 333; *305;*

- the inscription on the West Door of Moria, as mentioned above: in Elvish in the *Tengwar*, and in Elvish and English in the Roman alphabet;
- the inscription on Balin's tomb, in Daeron's Runes, in Westron (but readable as English) and in the Dwarves' tongue. (I, 416; *380*)

For the avid student of the languages and the calligraphy of Middle-earth nothing here can replace study of Tolkien's very detailed explanations in the Appendices. The information here only highlights some essentials from that mass of detail. If it can help the average reader make his or her way through Tolkien's story with greater ease and enjoyment, it has served a purpose.

Sixteen

MIND, SPIRIT, AND DREAM IN
THE LORD OF THE RINGS

This chapter attempts to deal with matters that run all through Tolkien's story, both on and below the surface, and which therefore cannot be assigned to a discussion of any specific episode in the narrative, or the development of any characters, or to the culture of Middle-earth itself. Yet these matters enrich and color and give tone and feeling to all else. The poems Tolkien wrote for his book, the spiritual perceptions of its characters (and, it may be diffidently stated, of its creator), and the vivid and useful dreams of those characters all provide texture and meaning to the world of Middle-earth.

POEMS AND SONGS

Tolkien said that the poems and songs in *The Lord of the Rings* were not there for their own sake, nor because of any intrinsic poetic merit, but for dramatic or narrative effect at the particular point of their appearance.[1] It would therefore seem that form and style should not matter much in the verse. Nonetheless, there is a wide variety of forms, types, and styles of poetry in the tale. Depending on how you count repetitions, reprises, and variants, there are between fifty and sixty examples of verse in *The Lord of the Rings*. They can be classified in several ways.

The most frequent verse form is the rhymed couplet, appearing in a number of different meters, with twenty-two examples. There are six examples of tetrameter quatrains (three of them variants of "The Road goes ever on and on"), six examples of Old English prosody (discussed below), four of ballad stanza, and seventeen or so of various nonce-forms of stanza, rhythm, or rhyme scheme.

The important thing to remember about these poems is that most aspire to the condition of song. Most of these verses are not in fact poems per se but song lyrics. Of the fifty and more sets of words which one could call verses, thirty-one are expressly said to be sung; a couple are chanted; several are recited (as by Sam, in his schoolroom manner, hands behind his back); and one exists, so to speak, only in writing (Snowmane's epitaph, which the text gives us, but which is not spoken by anyone).[2]

As for authorship, as might be expected in a book as hobbitocentric as this one, nineteen poems are by Hobbits, varying from Gollum's riddle of the fish (II, 288; *269*) to Bilbo's poem of Eärendil (I, 308-ll; *282–5*, at 124 lines almost twice as long as any other poem in the book), from bath songs to road songs, to Frodo's lament for Gandalf. (I, 465–6; *424–5*) Ten are Elvish in origin, some traditional ("A Elbereth Gilthoniel"), some composed by Galadriel, some by Legolas; two given in the original Elvish (in the Elvish language, Tolkien was indisputably the world's greatest poet). Six are from Ents, a couple from Tom Bombadil, one by Gimli, and one rather grisly piece is chanted by a Barrow-wight. The rest, including eight in the measure of Rohan (Old English verse) are contributed by Men, counting Gandalf in Man-form for this purpose. He speaks, if not originates, several (some of which he calls Rhymes of Lore); and Aragorn speaks, and apparently originates, several others.

Several modern poets, including writers like Richard Wilbur, have attempted to re-create or emulate Old English poetry, but none has been as successful as Tolkien in capturing both the prosody and the spirit of that verse. (Tolkien might indeed give praise to Seamus Heaney's new translation of *Beowulf*.) This poetry is characterized by a strong medial pause or caesura such that a line is in effect two half-lines, with four beats to a line, and heavy alliteration on each side of the pause:

Doom drove them on. Darkness took them,
horse and horseman; hoofbeats afar
sank into silence: so the songs tell us. (III, 92; *83*)

Here the pause is marked by actual punctuation in all three lines. The alliterating elements are the "d's," the "h's," and the "s's," and the stresses or beats can be variously read. One possible pattern is:

DOOM drove them ON. DARKness TOOK them,
HORSE and HORSEman; HOOFbeats aFAR
SANK into SIlence: SO the songs TELL us.

Plainly this is poetry meant to be recited aloud from memory, whether on a festal or a funereal occasion; it is poetry that is also record-keeping, a way of preserving history and lore. And indeed the Anglo-Saxon or Old English poetic tradition was an oral one, with bards, or *scops* (pronounced "shops") reciting in a meadhall like Meduseld or Heorot, probably for generations before a line of poetry was ever written down.

As conveyed by Tolkien, Old English is a poetry of somber celebration with a strongly fatalistic cast. It celebrates the deeds of Men (literally—it is the poetry of a warrior society), whether of martial ardor and impetus toward victory ("Arise, arise . . . ," see III, 137; *123*), or of loss ("Mourn not . . . ," see III, 145; *130*). Unlike Hobbit verse it is never light; unlike Elvish poetry it is often grim.

Excepting the unique properties of Old English verse, belonging mostly to Rohan, there seems to be little correlation between the origins of a poem and its form. That is, for instance, Elves as well as Hobbits can compose in ballad stanza, as a comparison of Bilbo's "I sit beside the fire . . ." (I, 364–5; *333–4*) with Legolas's "An Elvin-maid . . ." (I, 440–2; *401–3*) shows.

Most of the poems are occasional—they are written to celebrate or commemorate some specific occasion, whether it is a hot bath and its pleasures, or the bittersweetness of leaving Lothlórien, or the fateful ride of Théoden and the Rohirrim. They reflect or heighten the emotion of the occasion whatever it may be. In the case of Rohan they also record the historical impact of events. Other poems are occasional in a different way: they are helpful on a particular occasion, as is old Ioreth's rhyme about the use-fulness of *athelas* for the Black Breath, lines which the herb-master of the Houses of Healing wrongly dismisses as doggerel.

Still other poems verge on being riddles, or are highly cryptic, such as the words spoken by the voice in the dream that Faramir and Boromir had: "Seek for the Sword that was broken" (I, 323; *296*), or the words of Malbeth the Seer, which Elrond bid Aragorn remember at a particular moment; the passage is about the Paths of the Dead and the need to take that route. After Aragorn recites the lines, Gimli comments that the Paths themselves are no darker than the meaning of Malbeth's words (see III, 64; *58–9*).

And at least one poem serves as a kind of signal, when Sam is seeking Frodo in the Tower of Cirith Ungol and sings "In western lands . . ." and thinks he hears "a faint voice answering him." (III, 226; *204–5*)

In *The Lord of the Rings*, as in many other works of literature, music and poetry are the expressions of memory (looking back) and desire (looking forward). They are, that is, expressions of spirit. Much less obvious but equally valid as an expression of spirit is religion. Tolkien's faith or belief, and how it is rendered in *The Lord of the Rings*, has been the subject of much discussion.

TOLKIEN'S BELIEFS AND HIS BOOK[3]

There are no religious institutions in Middle-earth. With one possible exception there are no religious observances.[4] Yet, like his friend C. S. Lewis, Tolkien was a deeply religious man. He was raised in the Roman Catholic faith (his guardian for a time after his mother's death was a priest, Father Francis Morgan). He surely did not check his faith and belief at the door when he sat down to write. We must, however, look beneath the surface of the story to find its religious coloration, and to see if that coloration is specifically Christian.

At the root of Tolkien's conception of literary art is the belief that imagination is the gift of God. As God is Creator, Humankind is sub-creator, or secondary creator of imagined worlds. As Tolkien says in "On Fairy-stories," we have the power to "make . . . because we are made . . . in the image . . . of a Maker."[5]

Such theology as *The Lord of the Rings* embodies is conventional or traditional enough, at least as it concerns the nature of evil. Evil is a falling away from good, a negation of good, an absence, rather than a positive and original force in itself. "'For nothing is evil in the beginning,'" Elrond tells his council. (I, 351; *321*) Because evil is a negativity, it cannot create. It can only mock living forms, as Treebeard tells Merry and Pippin: Trolls and Orcs mock or parody Ents and Elves, respectively (see II, 113; *105*), and Frodo affirms that view of the Dark Lord's limitation much later in Mordor. Whether crude imitation or mockery, the products of that uncreating word, such as Orcs, demonstrate the profoundly anti-creative nature of evil.

Evil hates life. It especially hates free life, and its hatred takes minor forms like chopping down trees, and major forms like blighting whole regions so that they can no longer support life. The supreme evil in the Third Age of Middle-earth is Sauron, and we have seen how he swallows up other life, so that ancient kings are now wraiths, and the Mouth of Sauron has no name.

But for all his enormous ego and hunger, Sauron is essentially a negation. When Frodo sees the Eye in the Mirror of Galadriel, it is "a window into nothing." (I, 471; *430*) Because it is so absorbed in self, evil cannot imagine the other (imagination is a gift from God after all): Gandalf has counted all along on Sauron's inability to consider that, having the Ring, the West would not use it; that the Free Peoples would actually seek to destroy it Sauron cannot even begin to conceive (see II, 127; *119*).

This is all traditional enough; Sauron in these qualities has considerable resemblance to Milton's portrayal of Satan in the early books of *Paradise Lost*. At the same time, Tolkien takes care to eschew traditional Christian symbolism, especially figurations of Christ. If Christ is thought of as world-redeemer, his analogue might be Frodo, and Tolkien is careful to emphasize that Frodo failed. If Christ is thought of as resurrected deity, his analogue might be Gandalf, and Tolkien is careful to point out how impious the comparison would be.[6]

My own estimate, after some thinking, is that the book's essential religious nature and even its specifically Christian cast lie not in theology nor in symbolism but in emotion. And the emotions in which these matters are embodied are hope and despair.

Despair is briefly dealt with, especially since Gandalf forbade it. To despair is to commit an enormous act of pride or hubris, for it means seeing the end beyond all doubt, that is, being omniscient. To be disheartened and discouraged is a rather frequent state in the story, but only twice, I think, do we see actual despair; both instances are, as might be expected, rather late in the tale. Sam at the Black Gate of Mordor is in despair; Denethor during the Siege of Gondor likewise despairs (the two events, on opposite sides of the great River, occur as crisis deepens in each theatre of action and are only a few days apart). Sam despairs because of insufficient understanding, Denethor because he thinks he understands all too well.

Sam gives up hope: at the closed gate of Morannon, at what Sam perceives as "the bitter end" (II, 310; *289*); when what seems to be the only way into Mordor is barred against him and Frodo, despair covers Sam like a shroud.

Denethor, arguing about the disposition of the Ring, says he would not have put it "'at a hazard beyond all but a fool's hope'" (III, 105; *95*), courting utter disaster. (Denethor thinks ruin is imminent because he thinks the Seeing Stone has been telling him the entire truth. It has in fact been showing him only enough to make him think the West is losing.) In the Houses of the Dead Denethor cries to Gandalf, "'Pride and despair! . . . The West has failed.'" (III, 157; *142*)

And what happens in either case? Sam and Frodo go on; Sam even sees an oliphaunt (to his everlasting delight and terror), they meet Faramir, and they receive help and rest and counsel. Gondor is saved despite Denethor: Rohan comes, and the fleet of black sails his *palantír* has shown him is a squadron of friends, not enemies. Aragorn has come to relieve the siege.

As to hope, it does not inspire the actions east of the River Anduin. Frodo must struggle onward whether or not he feels hopeful about his eventual goal. But westward, in the manifold actions leading to the War of the Rings, where the forces of the Free Peoples must contend with the mighty forces of Sauron, hope can ebb and flow. In the early chapters of Books III and V hope seems to be a keyword, a theme, a recurrent notion, positively or negatively.

- Éomer says little hope remains of finding the hobbits when Aragorn explains his mission early in Book III.
- Gandalf returns and speaks hopefully about the future conduct of the campaign; but he cautions that hope is not certainty.
- When Théoden awakens and resumes his kingly mien, men feel hope for Rohan.
- Our hope is in the east, Gandalf tells the king.
- At Helm's Deep, Aragorn calls for stout defense of the citadel throughout the night: "'day will bring hope,'" he says. (II, 180; *167*)

Then, as war deepens at the opening of Book V:

- Beregond the guard questions if Gondor can withstand Sauron's attack. Yet even if we fall, he tells Pippin, "'Hope and memory shall live still.'" (III, 43–4; *40–1*)
- Arwen sends a message to Aragorn: *"'Either our hope cometh, or all hope's end.'"* (III, 56; *52*)

A concordance could list many more examples, but the point is sufficiently made: this is normal, rational hope, the kind of hope that good Men and Hobbits have; the kind that springs eternal in the human breast.

But the emotion ranges far above and beyond this level:

- Aragorn exclaims that Gandalf has returned "'beyond hope.'" (II, 125; *116*)
- When reinforcements (Théoden and Éomer and their troops) appear at Helm's Deep the guard calls it good news and repeats the very words. (II, 172; *159*)
- When later at Helm's Deep the Huorns obliterate the Orc army, Gandalf takes no credit; it was not his plan, he says, but it worked "'better even than my hope. . . . '" (II, 189; *175*).

In this question of hope and despair, certainly it is Christian—but not exclusively so—to put oneself lower than one's Creator, and not, by despairing, to set oneself equal to Him. But the idea of something happening "beyond hope," or something coming to pass which was only a "fool's hope" (as Denethor characterizes Gandalf's strategy) seems specifically Christian.

One can say—without prejudice—that the very nature of Christianity is exactly a "fool's hope." The redemption at the center of Christian belief is totally "beyond hope," beyond any rational expectation or probability. It is rationally absurd to suppose that God would become mortal, die, and rise from the dead for us; as Tertulian is said to have remarked, "I believe it *because* it is impossible."

What the Christian is called upon to believe is so far beyond the merely rational as to strain the faith, hope, credulity of any but a fool, just as anyone's belief that Frodo's errand will succeed and destroy Evil is beyond any probability. Robert M. Adams supposes he is offering an adverse criticism when he remarks that Frodo's action of carrying the Ring in the heart of Enemy country does not "really make much practical sense,"[7] but Frodo's action is well out of the reach of practical sense.

Yet Frodo's errand does succeed, so what happens then to rationality, and probability, and practical sense? They are superseded, just as the central miracle of Christianity supersedes historical probability in both the incarnation and the resurrection of Jesus Christ. The saving of Middle-earth is certainly not to be compared in significance to the saving of this world or of the individual soul. There may, however, be applicability (as Tolkien might say). Hope, even a fool's hope, may be justified.

THE LAND OF DREAMS

If in *The Lord of the Rings* poems can serve as a form of dramatic punctuation, and Frodo's journey can be a spiritual progress of a particular kind, then dreams can be symbols, images, and types of many kinds of emotions. Being unbounded by space, time, or probability, dreams can be very useful literary items, perhaps especially for writers of fantasy. There we can see dreams used as framing devices, as Alice dreams her adventures in *Alice in Wonderland;* or as plot devices, as Jane Studdock's veridical dreams initiate the action in C. S. Lewis's *That Hideous Strength,* or as purely symbolic devices, as Arren dreams in Ursula Le Guin's *The Farthest Shore* of a ruined cobweb-laden hall which stands for the death of magery in Earthsea.

Dreams can foreshadow, prophesy, echo, suggest, or even reveal. Given their evident literary value, and given the space available to him, Tolkien uses dreams with considerable restraint in *The Lord of the Rings.* There are eight fully or partially described dreams in the tale, and all except two of them were dreamed by a hobbit.

One of the exceptional dreams seems to be more a sending than a dream, and it came to Faramir often and to his brother Boromir once. In it the *eastern* sky grows dark, and a voice comes out of the still-lighted *West,* saying: "Seek for the Sword that was broken..." (see I, 323; *296* for the full stanza).

That the voice came from the West seems again to suggest the intervention, or at least the prompting, of the Valar. The various elements of the rhyme are explicated at the Council of Elrond. It is significant, perhaps, in the relationship of Faramir and Boromir that although Faramir was eager to seek Imladris, the place of the sword, Boromir prevailed with their father and came instead.

Among all the dreamers in the tale, Faramir perhaps occupies the oddest position. Not only does he often have the riddle-dream just mentioned, he also (as Tolkien's persona in part) dreams an Atlantean dream of Tolkien's own. Tolkien describes how from his earliest years he has had "a terrible recurring dream ... of the Great Wave, towering up, and coming in ineluctably over the trees and green fields."[8] Not only did his son Michael inherit this dream (though for years neither father nor son knew the other had had it), but Tolkien also gave it to Faramir.

Faramir describes the dream to Éowyn as they stand on the ramparts of the Houses of Healing looking northward. It is the very moment of Sauron's destruction; the air is unnaturally still, and they see a vast mountain of darkness rising. Faramir says that his recurring dream reminds him of Númenor, "'... of the great dark wave climbing over green lands ... and coming on, darkness inescapable.'" (III 297; *268*)

And yet, as Faramir knows and acknowledges, the dream is not evil: the dream is of the end of evil, whether seen as a picture of the destruction of corrupted Númenor, or as a picture of the fall of Sauron and his realm—ends of two evils that were worse for once having been good, and that were indissolubly linked: the end of the entity, Sauron, whose baleful influence had caused the end of the great kingdom, Númenor.

These dreams aside, all the others are dreamed by hobbits. They fall roughly into three groups: quasi-dreams, real dreams without detail, and real dreams with fairly complete circumstantiality, which serve various narrative purposes.

By quasi-dreams I mean mental phenomena that occur in the borderland between sleep and waking. On the way to the Ford of Bruinen, the wounded Frodo is "half in a dream" and imagining dark wings. (I, 273; *250*) In the Mines of Moria, Frodo thinks he's dreaming when he sees tiny lights (see I, 414; *379*). He is in fact awake, though drowsy, and is seeing Gollum's eyes in the dark. Similarly, Frodo is half-asleep on March 13 of the year after the Quest; he is ill and he is muttering about emptiness and the loss of "It." (III, 376; *339*) This small detail shows how profoundly the Ring and its loss have affected Frodo, although he usually has strength enough to put the loss aside.

Real dreams without detail include (among others) Frodo's therapeutic dream as he and Sam approach the Black Gate: no recollection of it stayed with him, but it made him feel happier (see II, 305–6; *285*). And as they near Mount Doom Frodo predictably has "dreams of fire." (III, 244; *220*)

Of the six real hobbit dreams described in greater or less detail, three belong to Frodo, and one each to Merry, Pippin, and Sam. Merry's dream, Pippin's dream, and two of Frodo's dreams take place in the house of Tom Bombadil.

The night before the hobbits are to set out for the Old Forest, Frodo dreams of a white tower that he longs to climb in order to look at the Sea; he is awakened before he can do so. (I, 154; *142*) This is presumably one of the Towers where Frodo and those riding with him as he leaves Middle-earth can look out to Sea as they proceed to Mithlond and the Grey Havens. (III, 383; *346*) It is the place among the Tower Hills, Gandalf told Pippin, where one of the Seeing Stones was located: near "'Mithlond . . . where the grey ships lie.'" (II, 259; *240*) If this is indeed the same place, the dream is the first in a pattern which hints at Frodo's ultimate fate.

The only other dream with any detail which takes place outside Tom Bombadil's realm is one Sam has as he, Frodo, and Gollum approach the Cross-roads in Ithilien. Sam dreams he is searching around in the garden back at Bag End; but the garden is all overgrown and unkempt, a weary task ahead for Sam. "Presently he remembered what he was looking for. 'My pipe!' he said, and . . . woke up." (II, 391; *363–4*) Given the hobbits' situation, this seems a commonplace, but appropriate, anxiety dream. Sam has already seen in the Mirror of Galadriel that destruction is going on in the Shire, which someone will have to set to rights; and he is very tired; their journey has already been arduous although the worst remains ahead. It is a very probable sort of dream to be having at this point.

We are left then with the dreams in Tom Bombadil's house. Understandably, Pippin dreams of being shut up in Old Man Willow again, whereas Merry dreams of water, water "rising slowly but surely"; he imagines drowning. (I, 178; *164*) This may be a precognitive dream, referring to the future occasion when the Ents flood Isengard. When that happened, Merry later tells his friends that "'the water was rising rapidly'" but he and Pippin found a safely elevated spot and watched the water pour in. (II, 225; *208*)

If Merry's dream is precognitive, there may be something even more peculiar than first appears about Tom Bombadil's little land. It is a place, as we have seen, where the Ring's power is strangely limited or skewed: neither Tom nor Frodo disappears from the other's sight when wearing the Ring.

And Tom has some kind of power over time: he takes the entranced hobbits in narrative back "into times when the world was wider. . . ." (I, 182; *168*) Tom's language (and it is a matter of language) has power over time in that way, being able to take the hobbits back to when the West was not inaccessible to ordinary beings, and in another way, for when he was done, Frodo and his friends could not tell whether hours or perhaps days had passed, so great was the charm of his words.

In a realm like this, it is no wonder that one night Frodo can dream of the past, seeing Gandalf on the Tower of Orthanc, which the wizard had left a week earlier (see Chapter 4), *and* the next night he can dream of a song like a light behind a curtain, and the curtain rolling back, at which "a far green country opened before him under a swift sunrise." (I, 187; *172*) Tom's strange little land seems to be a place where time is highly pliable, or where, in dreams at least, one can look through windows opening on either past or future.

A land of dream indeed: the dream of the green country is, in terms of Frodo's life, a dream of the far future, when Frodo arrives in Elvenhome or Eressëa, and "as in his dream in the house of Bombadil . . . he beheld a far green country under a swift sunrise." (III, 384; *347*) But also, because Elvenhome was removed from the Circle of the World at the end of the Second Age, this is a dream beyond the time of this world, and—even this early in Frodo's Quest—a dream foretelling reward after the suffering of life within Middle-earth.

Seventeen

HOBBITS IN HOLLYWOOD: THE *FELLOWSHIP* FILM

J. R. R. Tolkien reportedly sold the film rights to *The Lord of the Rings* five years before his death for the inconsiderable sum of £10,000 (more considerable, perhaps, in 1968, but still not munificent).[1] The chain of custody of those rights is complex, but has ended, as we all know, with New Line Cinema and Peter Jackson making three feature-length films, corresponding to the three parts of Tolkien's epic tale. The first of these, *The Fellowship of the Ring*, was released in December 2001.

Tolkien himself was apparently of two minds about the possibility of converting print to celluloid. When an American film company proposed an animated version back in 1957 Tolkien wrote to his publisher that "I should welcome the idea of an animated motion picture. . . ."[2] However, when the actual synopsis or "story-line," as he called it, came into his hands Tolkien wrote that he felt "very unhappy about the extreme silliness and incompetence" of the text.[3] Nothing came of this project in any case, and no full-scale effort to put *The Lord of the Rings* on the screen occurred until Peter Jackson and his associates came along in the late 1990s. (Ralph Bakshi's misguided 1978 attempt is best passed over in silence.)

Nothing in the world of cinema or law is ever simple, of course. That Tolkien sold his rights as just described has been the received wisdom on the subject for many years. But just as Peter Jackson's film opened in Great

Britain, the lore was called into question. In the *Guardian* of December 11, 2001, Fiachra Gibbons writes as follows:

> Tolkien, who despite his donnish image was a canny old fox when it came to money, negotiated a pretty lucrative long-term deal when he finally sold the movie rights to the *Ring* in 1969.
>
> Far from the £10,000 of lore, he got $250,000 (then worth about £102,500) and a percentage of the royalties, which could eventually be a massive fillip to his estate, already fat from the sale of 100m books around the globe. The estate's solicitors confirmed yesterday that it would get more royalties if the film took two and a half times its costs.[4]

Although the Tolkien family has had no control over the course of events in filmdom, its reaction to the movie project has been interesting. Christopher Tolkien, Tolkien's son and literary executor, has been quarreling with his own son, Simon, over whether or not he (Christopher) approved of the idea of filming the tale, and over Simon's seeming enthusiasm for the film proposal. Simon and *his* son, age 11, have apparently been banished from the family circle, and Simon, a barrister, has been excluded from any role in the governance of his grandfather's estate.[5] It all seems rather Orkish.

Many of the basic facts about Peter Jackson's grand attempt are well-known: that he himself is a devoted *LOTR* fan, that a great deal of consultation with other Tolkien fans world-wide took place during shooting, that all three films were shot more or less at once and, regardless of release date, are now complete, that the project cost something like $270 million dollars, and that the film (the first installment anyway) has become a major box office success.

Less well-known is that great care was exercised in creating the material world of the film: its swords and armor, its costuming, the banners and insignia of its multitudinous military forces; craftspeople were at work in the spirit of the Elves and Dwarves of Middle-earth itself.

Also little known, but perhaps even more gratifying, is that publicity for the film has led back to vastly greater sales for the books. *The Fellowship of the Rings* alone sold six times as many copies in 2001 as in 2000 (1.8 million compared to 600,000).[6]

Interestingly, the *Fellowship* film, as a film, is also a creative success: Many who have never read *The Lord of the Rings,* or who have only vaguely heard of Tolkien himself, have been enthralled by what they have seen on the screen. But the question that interests lovers of Tolkien's work most is, how successful is the film in comparison to what Tolkien wrote? To that vexed matter, as you might suppose, there have been nearly as many reactions as readers. Here is a composite of some conversations that I have heard.

Why did they omit the Old Forest/Tom Bombadil/Barrow-downs episodes?

The first thing that constrained the filmmakers was time: The film is almost three hours long as it is, and some difficult choices had to be made. One could argue about the correctness of any of them, but the omission of Tom and by extension of the episodes to which he is central is defensible. Even Tolkien noted that Tom doesn't quite seem to fit: as an artistic representation, he had been developed independently of hobbits and Rings. Tom is there as a "comment," as Tolkien told Naomi Mitchison (see Chapter 3), and what he seems to be a comment on is the impossibility of neutrality or indifference, the impossibility of being in any sense above the struggle, in a world-wide conflict where everything is at stake. Tom can claim to be indifferent to the politics of Middle-earth, but Tolkien meant his presence to show that one cannot live unto oneself when life itself will fail if Evil wins.

So Tom does represent an important idea, but also a turning aside from the central line of the story's development; the main problem of his omission is that the historical importance of the weapons he provided the younger hobbits on the Barrow-downs must be shown by other means. (No sword but the one Merry wielded could have slain the Captain of the Nazgûl, and so on.)

There is too much violence on the screen.

Unfortunate, if true. But we live in a media-molded age in which violence is portrayed everywhere. It is one of the liabilities of transferring representations of action from words to images that they appear by definition more graphic. The body-count in Tolkien is quite high, the descriptions are quite vivid, the attacks and counter-attacks and murderous set-tos are pretty frequent: the difference is that in reading you can skip or skim. But Tolkien's text is not afraid to depict violence directly, and the film is thus not untrue to the spirit of the tale.

Too much is made of Saruman in this segment of the film.

Again, it's a question of having to make choices. It makes sense to *show* Saruman's treachery to Gandalf and his general betrayal of the Free Peoples, rather than to have Gandalf *tell* of these things, as in the text he does at the Council of Elrond. It is one of the interesting examples of how a narrative form can be converted to a dramatic form. One might protest that the duel arcane that takes place between the two wizards is overdone, and it is certainly unsupported by anything in the text, but it is more an extreme of representation than any actual misrepresentation. (More misleading is that Saruman continues to wear white, a color which in the text he has abandoned for parti-colored robes in the course of his falling into evil.)

Also questionable is the time spent portraying the development of the Uruk-Hai, Saruman's fierce Orcs of the White Hand, considering that they are to be wiped out in the next book of the tale. Still there is a horrid fascination in watching Saruman's misuse of power to fabricate these creatures rising (like Adam? like a golem?) from the clay.

Arwen Evenstar has been turned into a warrior princess.

This change may be a bow to commercial necessity. It is certainly true that almost every group of students or other readers notice the lack of female roles in Tolkien's work. I have tried to explain this a little in Chapter 13 by suggesting that women have unobtrusive, but not unimportant, places in this masculine world of rough adventure: They wait, they maintain ordinary life, they preserve beauty and goodness wherever they can.

Arwen's role is thus an acknowledgement of present-day audience expectations. The substitution is unfortunate for the admirable Glorfindel, but

Liv Tyler performs her role with grace and panache. And the love story of Arwen and Aragorn, while highlighted more than in Tolkien's words, is by no means distorted.

Very well, you have tried to meet some negative criticisms. Have you any negative criticisms of your own?

Yes, but they are comparatively minor, and come from a frame of mind that says you aren't doing your job unless you find *some* fault. To nit-pick: I find Gimli's saying at the Bridge of Khazad-dûm that "Nobody tosses a dwarf" startlingly inappropriate. It may be a throwaway line, it may be a sort of inside joke, but it clearly refers to dwarf-tossing as a sport practiced in various bars in Australia and elsewhere, and it breaks the frame badly.

Objections to the handling of the Council of Elrond may be less trivial. Rivendell is a building, not a village. The Council takes place indoors, not outdoors. There are not a lot of unnamed figures sitting about in the Middle-earth equivalent of camp chairs. Most of all, the Council does not end in rancorous quarreling: as debate winds down, the Council sits "with downcast eyes" in a profound silence until Frodo can speak his poignant words.

But these cavils about the Council amount to my interpretation versus the director's, one vision of a particular narrative moment opposed to another. They do not vitiate the film's overall power.

Given all that, what positive comments can you make about the film?

Several. Most notably, two huge things stand out in my mind: the casting and the setting.

Having already spoken of Liv Tyler, and meaning no disrespect to any other fine performer, let me mention just three excellent casting choices:[7]

- Sean Bean as Boromir: Tolkien always mentioned the mixed and complex nature of the Man of Gondor when people accused him of creating only black-and-white characters. Bean brings out very well the bravery and selflessness of Boromir, while at the same time showing his intermittent lust for power, his egotism, and with all these, his sense of his own unworthiness when those less admirable traits come to the fore. Boromir loves the hobbits at the same time he lusts for the Ring; these are contradictory drives, both of which are destructive. He redeems himself at last.

- Viggo Mortensen as Aragorn: seeing this actor come into his own in a heroic role was a pleasant surprise; I had seen Mortensen only as the sleazy artist/con man in Michael Douglas's *A Perfect Murder*. Here he brought out both the roughness and the regal quality of a man who has ranged the wild for many years and is also heir presumptive to a throne. He conveys the nobility latent in Aragorn, a quality that rough clothing and weather-beaten countenance cannot wholly conceal.

- Sir Ian McKellen as Gandalf: Even more than Frodo's, this was the one role that had to be right. And McKellen, one of the great actors in the English-speaking world, was right and got it right. Until his fall in Moria, Gandalf is the power, the glue if you will, that holds everything together, and McKellen embodies the wisdom and humanity that Gandalf must show. By turns compassionate, angry, tough-minded, tender-hearted, Gandalf is the only character (except perhaps Elrond) who understands at the deepest level the significance of the Quest that is being undertaken. As played by McKellen, Gandalf shows Frodo that more is involved here than doing one's duty: At the last extremity, one must sacrifice oneself.

As to the setting: New Zealand. Aside from being Peter Jackson's native land, New Zealand seems a perfect milieu for a film set in Middle-earth. It is sparsely enough settled to be reminiscent of the rural England Tolkien remembered from boyhood, on which locales like the Shire are based. In climate it is congruent to the north Temperate Zone. Its landforms, from snow-clad mountains to blue lakes to lush green fields, have the variety that the landscapes of Middle-earth have. At the same time, it is different: As we move out from the Shire, places become enough *unlike* England (or our ideas of England) to let us believe we are in another time and a wider world. There is subtle unfamiliarity, and at the same time a sense of rightness in the appearance of landscapes and scenes. Certainly as the travelers set out from Lothlórien down the Great River, what I see (in the long overhead shot) is just what I imagined. I said to myself, "That's exactly what it looks like."

Even allowing for the sophistication of special visual effects, and for all that is artificial (such as the constructed village that Rivendell seems to be) enough is authentic in the visual world of the film to earn the approval of even quite critical viewers.

The reactions of reviewers have been among the most interesting phenomena of the film's release. The reviews range from the idiotic (those which speak of "sequels" to *The Fellowship,* thus betraying a complete failure to understand the structure of either the book or the film) through the merely banal ("epic sweep" and so forth) to the genuinely thoughtful. The most thoughtful comments have come from writers who create a kind of triangular configuration between themselves, the film, and the Tolkien text; to make their observations still more complex these writers have divided "themselves" into adult writers of today and their younger selves as readers of *The Lord of the Rings.* Two examples must suffice.

Anthony Lane writes in *The New Yorker* before having seen the film.[8] Anticipation of its release has led him to write an essay in which he reflects on Tolkien and his career, on the admiration (and denigration) *The Lord of the Rings* has elicited over the generations, and on his own reaction to the rather overwhelming experience of reading Tolkien in his twelfth and thirteenth years. "It was," he says, "a book that happens to you: a chunk bitten out of your life." Citing Tolkien's remark in his "Foreword" that "This tale grew in the telling," Lane adds, "more significantly, the reader grows in the reading; such is the source of Tolkien's power, and it is weirder and more far-reaching than even he could have imagined."

So Lane looks forward to the film with a mixture of happy anticipation and real trepidation. Having originally read the book at an age to be properly enchanted by it, and having now in his adult sophistication discerned its gross faults of ambitious scope and elevated rhetoric (what some call its faults, a line of criticism which Tolkien would implacably ignore), he cannot but wonder what the film will be like. Lane does not minimize Tolkien's real power: What he seems to do, a sadder thing altogether, is patronize his younger self, and condescend to his own youthful imagination.

Louis Menand in *The New York Review of Books* is in a similar situation.[9] He too read *The Lord of the Rings* when he was eleven, and it acted powerfully on his imagination in various ways: He remembers it, he says, "as an eleven-year-old's Proust." This is a scary comparison: It implies that, at eleven, Menand had already read Proust so he could make, and remember, that comparison. I don't think he meant that.

But Menand writes as one who has in fact seen the film. And he took the precaution of bringing with him a fourteen-year-old who had recently read the book (a boy, of course) to get a view through fresh and unjaded eyes. Unfortunately, Menand notes that the fourteen-year-old of today is probably jaded in a way that a fourteen-year-old reader in, say, 1955, could not have been. Menand characterizes his own original reaction as essentially naïve. Again, he seems to be looking down on his earlier self, not with scorn certainly, but with a kind of gentle amusement at such gullibility. (What actually seems naïve, or at least forgetful, is the assumption that a youngster of the 1950s would be visually innocent: Was there not Walt Disney? Were not comic books so violent and so plentiful as to panic "experts" in child psychology?)

At any rate, the comparisons implicit in such discussions between what the author was trying to do, and what the filmmaker was trying to do, and between the receptive imagination in youth and in middle age are highly instructive. They show both how powerful Tolkien's art has been, and how difficult it is anatomize one's own memories of that power. They ought to teach us to temper our own appraisals, and to forgive the appraisals of others.

On March 24, 2002, *The Lord of the Rings: The Fellowship of the Ring* won four Academy Awards. The Oscars were given for best original musical score (the work of Howard Shore), best make-up, best visual effects, and best cinematography. These were not glamorous individual awards, but they suggest the great extent to which the making of the film was an ensemble or collaborative effort. They laud the accomplishments which made the world—and made a believable world—in which the Quest could take place. In any event, this first part of *The Lord of the Rings* has been in theaters for about three months, and the trailer for the second part, *The Two Towers,* is about to appear. The quality of the first part gives us reason to hope for the value of the next two. At the same time, the changes in Tolkien's story, whether forced upon the filmmakers, or decided on for aesthetic reasons, have to give us pause. Tolkien's story is closely enough plotted so that changing it can build in more and more distortion. Will the changes already made necessitate greater changes later and have the cumulative effect of making the film less and less like Tolkien as it continues? (Rumor is already rife, for instance, that the Scouring of the Shire will be omitted.)

Whatever answers this question turns out to have, we can at least be sure that we have been in the presence of one of the largest filmmaking enterprises of our time. It is a major effort, undertaken with love, and care, and knowledge, and (not to be despised) plenty of money. Much is always lost in translation, but in this translation, much is also preserved.

AFTERWORD

Most of what I have written here has been descriptive or explanatory. I have tried to show some of the ways in which *The Lord of the Rings* works, in terms of story, character, theme, language, literary art, and so on. While it must be clear that I think that Tolkien's tale is superb of its kind, I have avoided evaluation as such.

No longer. Since I have devoted many working days and years to reading it, and teaching it, and (now) writing about it, it should come as no surprise when I say that I think *The Lord of the Rings* is the finest work of heroic fantasy in the language. It is the standard by which all other works in this vein should be measured.

This is not to say that other fantasy tales should be *like The Lord of the Rings*. God forbid. A whole class of imitators has sprung up since Tolkien's book gained its American popularity in the late 1960s, and those trying to be most like it are the worst: a few unpronounceable names, a few artifacts like swords or bracelets, a map (there must be maps), a good deal of wretched prose, and we suddenly have Middle-earth as trailer park.

There are honorable exceptions. Those fantasies which develop their own fully imagined worlds, and speak of those worlds in language as rich and supple as Tolkien's, are fit to hold their own with *The Lord of the Rings*, however different the contents of their worlds, and the style of their language, may be. One obviously praiseworthy example would be Ursula Le Guin's Earthsea tales; of quite recent vintage among thoroughly enchanting, and somber, fantasies is Philip Pullman's trilogy of *His Dark Materials*. And at least one reader's pleasure and profit have been enhanced by the work of writers as different as Joy Chant, Susan Cooper, John Crowley, and Alan Garner.

To honor Tolkien in this way is not to say that *The Lord of the Rings* is perfect. I am glad it is not. Tolkien was such a perfectionist that had he waited until his tale was entirely satisfactory (to him) we might never have gotten it, as we did not get *The Silmarillion* in his lifetime. Some things here are not adequately dealt with. We would like to know something about the two missing wizards; we would have been glad to go and see what remains of that great stronghold Osgiliath; Círdan the Shipwright seems too important a character, as the original holder of one of the Three Rings, to have only four words to say in the entire story.

All three of these criticisms go to the criticism of the basic fault in the story, which Tolkien himself pointed out, and which I have already mentioned: the book is too short. In *The Lord of the Rings* twentieth-century literature has a great treasure; it is no doubt a fundamental flaw of human nature always to wish for more. But we do.

Notes

NOTES TO CHAPTER 1

1. For biographical details, see Humphrey Carpenter, *Tolkien: A Biography* (Boston: Houghton Mifflin, 1977); hereafter cited as Carpenter.
2. Humphrey Carpenter, ed., *The Letters of J. R. R. Tolkien* (Boston: Houghton Mifflin, 1981), p. 288; hereafter cited as *Letters*.
3. J. R. R. Tolkien, *The Lord of the Rings* (New York: Ballantine, 1965), Part I, xi; 11. Hereafter references to the text of *The Lord of the Rings* will be incorporated in my text in parentheses showing part (or "volume") number I, II, III and page (normal face type for 1965 paperback edition; *italics* for the reset 1993 paperback edition).
4. *Letters*, p. 219.
5. Ruth Noel, in *The Languages of Tolkien's Middle-earth* (Boston: Houghton Mifflin, 1980), counts fourteen invented languages, not all of them of course fully developed in the course of *The Lord of the Rings;* hereafter cited as Noel, 1980.
6. See *Letters*, pp. 362 and 366.
7. Quoted in Carpenter, p. 126.
8. Quoted in Carpenter, p. 133.
9. This account is apocryphal, although Tolkien gives it in *Letters*, pp. 215 and 219; for variant versions of the origin of "hobbit" see Carpenter, pp. 176–177.
10. Carpenter, p. 179.
11. *Letters*, p. 218.
12. Cited in Carpenter, p. 176.
13. See Paul Kocher, *Master of Middle-earth* (Boston: Houghton Mifflin, 1972), p. 20; hereafter cited as Kocher.
14. Carpenter, p. 188.
15. For a detailed account of how *The Lord of the Rings* was composed and finally saw print, see Carpenter, pp. 183–218.
16. *Letters*, pp. 216–217.

NOTES TO CHAPTER 2

1. J. R. R. Tolkien, "On Fairy-Stories" in *The Tolkien Reader* (New York: Ballantine, 1966), p. 9.
2. Kocher, p. 2.
3. Tolkien himself identified Ursa Major for us; the other astronomical data are suggested in Kocher, p. 7.
4. The best treatment of *The Lord of the Rings* from the point of view of Quest and Quest-Hero—and one of the best essays on Tolkien's tale in general—is written by a former student of his: W. H. Auden, "The Quest Hero," *Texas Quarterly*, IV (1962), 81–93; rpt. in Neil Isaacs and Rose Zimbardo, eds., *Tolkien and the Critics* (Notre Dame, IN: University of Notre Dame Press, 1968), pp. 40–61.
5. The myth of creation is given in the "Ainulindalë" and "Valaquenta" sections of *The Silmarillion* (Boston: Houghton Mifflin, 1977), pp. 15–32.
6. *Letters*, p. 219. The emphasis is Tolkien's.
7. Cited in Jeffrey Henning, "Growing Up with Language," *Model Languages* vol. I, no. 8 (January-February 1996). This essay was e-mailed to me by a colleague; it and the journal in which it appeared can be found on line at www.langmaster.com. The essay is one of the better discussions I have read on the subject of invented languages, model languages, and the development of Tolkien's own families of languages. For other treatments see the Noel book cited above, and Tolkien's own "Guide to the Names in the Lord of the Rings," originally a series of notes Tolkien made to assist translators of his work. It was revised by Christopher Tolkien and appears in Jared Lobdell, ed., *A Tolkien Compass* (LaSalle, IL: Open Court, 1975), pp. 151–201; hereafter cited as *A Tolkien Compass*.

Unfortunately for Tolkien's lifelong passion for accuracy, error creeps in everywhere: readers of the current paperback edition will not find "omentielvo" at p. 110 of Part I; rather they will find "omentilmo."

NOTES TO CHAPTER 3

1. *Letters*, p. 288.
2. For a detailed discussion of this pattern, see David M. Miller, "Narrative Pattern in *The Fellowship of the Ring*," in *A Tolkien Compass*.
3. *Letters*, p. 26.
4. *Letters*, pp. 178–9.

NOTES TO CHAPTER 4

1. This is a point strongly pressed by W. H. Auden in the essay mentioned above.
2. See *Paradise Lost*, Book I *passim;* and see the discussion of Satan's ego in *A Preface to Paradise Lost* (London: Oxford UP, 1942) by Tolkien's friend and

colleague and fellow-Inkling, C. S. Lewis. It is difficult for *me* to imagine that these two men did not discuss Satanic and Sauronic evil in those days.

3. See *Letters,* p. 197.

NOTES TO CHAPTER 5

1. These laws, and the following discussions of governing proverbs and of parallelism between Books I and II, are adapted from Chapter 4, "Tolkien's World," in Randel Helms, *Tolkien's World* (Boston: Houghton Mifflin, 1974).

2. What Helms says about these proverbs needs heavy qualification; some of the governing sayings he identifies are not proverbial even in the world of Middle-earth. For a more detailed discussion of proverbial language, see my "'Advice is a Dangerous Gift': (Pseudo)Proverbs in *The Lord of the Rings,*" *Proverbium* 13 (1996): 331–346.

NOTES TO CHAPTER 6

1. See Helms, p. 92.
2. See Helms, p. 96.
3. See my essay already mentioned, or F. P. Wilson, ed., *The Oxford Dictionary of English Proverbs,* 3rd. edn. (Oxford: Clarendon Press, 1970), p. 753.
4. *Letters,* p. 237.

NOTES TO CHAPTER 7

1. *Letters,* p. 79.
2. See Ruth S. Noel, *The Mythology of Middle-earth* (Boston: Houghton Mifflin, 1978), p. 78.
3. See Helms, p. 99.

NOTES TO CHAPTER 8

1. See Helms, pp. 100 ff. for commentary on the roles of Pippin and Merry and their parallel actions in taking service with Denethor and Théoden.

2. I know that Éowyn and Éomer are Théoden's niece and nephew; but they were orphaned, and he was a widower; he reared them as his own children. See III, 437; *398–9.*

3. Further irony comes from the Classical allusion implied here: when Theseus returned to Athens, his fleet still bore black sails which he had forgotten to change; seeing them his father committed suicide, thinking Theseus dead. See *The Oxford Classical Dictionary* (Oxford: Clarendon Press, 1950), p. 10.

4. *Macbeth,* 4.1.80–81 and 5.8.15–16.

NOTES TO CHAPTER 9

1. See *Letters,* p. 236, for Tolkien's own eloquent exposition of Frodo's position.
2. My own candidate is Prince Imrahil of Dol Amroth. When I bring up his name, someone inevitably says, "Who?" thus making my point. Imrahil is of high blood (III, 23; *23*); his aunt or great-aunt was Denethor's wife; thus he is Faramir's cousin. He brings the most troops to defend Gondor. It is he who discovers that Éowyn is still alive on the battlefield; he takes command of the defense of Minas Tirith; he is stated to be the equal of Aragorn and Éomer (III, 167; *151*); he rules the city in Faramir's absence; he participates in the Last Debate, and he is with the king at Aragorn's entry into the city.
3. *Letters,* p. 198. In marrying Aragorn, Arwen had to renounce her right to go to Eldamar. That she was entitled to turn that right over to another is a matter of some doubt: see Tolkien's discussion of the question in *Letters,* pp. 327–9.
4. *Letters,* p. 328.
5. Letter to William Smith, January 9, 1795, as cited in Emily Beck, ed., *Familiar Quotations . . . by John Bartlett,* 14th edn. (Boston: Little, Brown, 1968), p. 454.
6. See his letter to Naomi Mitchison, quoted in Chapter 3.

NOTE TO INTRODUCTION TO PART II

1. Christopher Tolkien, ed., *Unfinished Tales* (Boston: Houghton Mifflin, 1980), p. 228.

NOTES TO CHAPTER 10

1. Carpenter, pp. 53, 103–4.
2. *Letters,* p. 176.
3. For a good graphic representation of the kinds of Elves and of their journeyings, see *The Silmarillion,* p. 309.
4. See Robert Foster, *The Complete Guide to Middle-earth* (New York: Ballantine, 1979), p. 85; hereafter cited as Foster.

NOTES TO CHAPTER 11

1. *Letters,* p. 207 and p. 383. Both letters discuss the same difficulty as Tolkien mentioned with "elves": trying to find English or "real-world" words that would not be misleading in describing his characters.
2. For this demographic information and more, see *The Lord of the Rings* "Appendix A," III, 438–51; *400–13*).
3. See *The Silmarillion,* especially Chapter 2. Subsequent chapters give further accounts of Elf-Dwarf quarrels.

NOTES TO CHAPTER 12

1. *Letters*, pp. 211–12 and 334.
2. *Letters*, p. 208.
3. *Letters*, p. 212.
4. *Letters*, p. 445.
5. *Letters*, p. 334. The place-names Treebeard mentions in his chant (Tasarinan, etc.) were all in Beleriand.
6. *Letters*, p. 335. The Dwarf creation is discussed in the previous chapter and in Chapter 2 of *The Silmarillion*.
7. *Letters*, p. 179.
8. *Letters*, p. 419.
9. Although Tolkien reports both that the Ents came suddenly and unbidden to his artistic imagination, and that he did not work on Book III where they appear until at least 1942 (see "Foreword," ix; *9*), in *The Return of the Shadow* (Boston: Houghton Mifflin, 1988), Christopher Tolkien tells us that a narrative fragment containing the conversation at the *Green Dragon* about "Tree-men" appears among very early versions of the first chapter of *The Fellowship of the Rings* (p. 254). Thus, Tolkien had "Tree-Men" of some sort on his mind well before he wrote Book III, but the specifics of "Ents" may not have come up until then. At any rate, it has to be pointed out that as the passage stands the chap who sighted the "Tree-Man" wandering in the North-farthing is called "Halfast," which is perhaps an example of what Tolkien called his "simple" but "tiresome" sense of humor (see Chapter 3 above).

NOTES TO CHAPTER 13

1. Some of the ideas in this chapter are from Paul Kocher, especially his Chapters V and VI, and from Deborah Rogers, "Everyclod and Everyhero: the Image of Man in Tolkien," in *The Tolkien Compass*, pp. 69–76.
2. C. S. Lewis, *Out of the Silent Planet* (New York: Avon, 1949), p. 102.
3. *Letters*, p. 232.
4. Kocher, p. 128.
5. This nice formulation paraphrases Deborah Rogers in the essay mentioned above (p. 73 in *The Tolkien Compass*).

NOTES TO CHAPTER 14

1. See *Letters*, p. 177.
2. *Unfinished Tales* gives the name of one Ring-wraith as Khamûl, second to the Captain; in this early treatment he was apparently the one who spoke to Gaffer Gamgee and was nosing about at the Bucklebury Ferry (pp. 338, 344).
3. *The Hobbit*, pp. 105–7.
4. "Fire take the werewolf-host!" according to Ruth Noel, 1980 (p. 38).

5. *Letters,* pp. 177–8.
6. See *Letters,* p. 190.
7. *The Silmarillion,* p. 50.
8. *Letters,* p. 180.
9. Foster, p. 445.
10. See *The Silmarillion.* p. 81.

NOTES TO CHAPTER 15

1. Resources for study of Tolkien's languages are copious and various: of first importance is Part III of *The Lord of the Rings,* especially Appendix E, "Writing and Spelling," and Appendix F, "The Languages and Peoples of the Third Age." Also of value are Ruth Noel, *The Languages of Tolkien's Middle-earth,* Jeffrey Henning's essay, and Tolkien's essay on translation in *A Tolkien Compass.* See the Bibliography.
2. *Letters,* p. 176.
3. *Letters,* p. 219.
4. Noel, 1980, pp. 37–39.
5. Noel, 1980, pp. 22–29.
6. Noel does not mention these utterances, probably for the reason given in the next paragraph of the text.
7. Among his linguistic enterprises, Tolkien expended considerable energy on the Book of Mazarbul, in creating those blackened and burnt pages, which he described as "facsimiles" or as work he had "forged." He wanted them to be frontispieces or at least illustrations in the first published editions of *The Lord of the Rings.* (See his notes to Rayner Unwin in *Letters,* pp. 170–1). To a later correspondent he drafted a letter that tells how he had to abandon the project because of production constraints. Christopher Tolkien notes that these facsimile pages were finally reproduced in *Pictures by J. R. R. Tolkien,* 1979. See *The Peoples of Middle-earth,* ed. Christopher Tolkien (Boston: Houghton Mifflin, 1996). They actually first appeared as the December page in the Tolkien Calendar for 1977, published by George Allen & Unwin.
8. See *Letters,* p. 125 and p. 132.

NOTES TO CHAPTER 16

1. He is quoted as saying that "a lot of the criticism of the verses shows a complete failure to understand the fact that they are all dramatic verses; they were conceived as the kind of things people would say under the circumstances." See Daniel Grotta-Kurska, *J. R. R. Tolkien: Architect of Middle-earth* (Philadelphia: Running Press, 1976), pp. 117–8.
2. An association item of some interest is the Caedmon recording of several Tolkien poems as set to music by the British comedian/composer Donald

Swann. They are sung by the wonderfully named British tenor William Elven; the disc includes Tolkien himself reciting "A Elbereth Gilthoniel" and a setting of Galadriel's Farewell suggested by Tolkien.

3. Religion and myth have received a great deal of attention from readers and critics of Tolkien; I do not therefore apologize for the scant treatment here. People more capable of belief than I am have written learnedly, indeed movingly, about Tolkien's spirituality. See, for instance, Verlyn Flieger's *A Question of Time* and Joseph Pearce's *Tolkien: Man and Myth,* both listed in the Bibliography. William Dowie's essay in the Salu and Farrell collection, and Chapter 3 of Lobdell's *England and Always* are also helpful, as are Tolkien's own letters, especially to Father Robert Murray.

4. The exception: Faramir and his men face west "in a moment of silence" before their meal in Henneth Annûn. They are in effect saying grace, as noted in Chapter 2.

5. *The Tolkien Reader,* p. 55.

6. For these considerations of Frodo and Gandalf, see *Letters,* p. 326 and 237 respectively.

7. Robert M. Adams, "The Hobbit Habit," *The New York Review of Books,* November 24, 1977; rpt. in Neil Isaacs and Rose Zimbardo, eds., *Tolkien: New Critical Perspectives* (Lexington, KY: The University Press of Kentucky, 1981), pp. 168–79.

8. *Letters,* p. 213 and note.

NOTES TO CHAPTER 17

1. See *Locus,* Vol. 48, No. 1 (Jan. 2002), p. 9.

2. Humphrey Carpenter, ed., *The Letters of J. R. R. Tolkien* (Boston: Houghton Mifflin, 1981), p. 257; hereafter cited as *Letters.*

3. *Letters,* p. 267.

4. "'Unworldly' Tolkien's ring of gold," *The Guardian,* http://film.guardian.co.uk/lordoftherings.news/ December 11, 2001.

5. *Locus,* p. 9, citing stories in the London newspaper, *The Independent.*

6. *Locus,* p. 9.

7. I will confine my negative views on the casting to a note: Elrond is improperly cast. Hugo Weaving is doubtless a fine actor, but he is made to look like an unhappy younger cousin of Willie Nelson's. Elves, even male Elves, are supposed to be beautiful. For general bearing, and for masculine attractiveness of feature, someone like the Peter Graves of the first *Mission Impossible* would have been preferable.

8. See Anthony Lane, "The Hobbit Habit," *The New Yorker,* December 10, 2001, pp. 98–105.

9. See Louis Menand, "Goblin Market," *The New York Review of Books,* January 17, 2002, pp. 8–9.

BIBLIOGRAPHY

Becker, Alida, ed. *The Tolkien Scrapbook.* New York: Grosset and Dunlap, 1978.

Carpenter, Humphrey. *The Inklings: C. S. Lewis, J. R. R. Tolkien, Charles Williams, and Their Friends.* Boston: Houghton Mifflin, 1979.

———. *Tolkien: A Biography.* Boston: Houghton Mifflin, 1977.

Carpenter, Humphrey, ed. *The Letters of J. R. R. Tolkien.* Boston: Houghton Mifflin, 1981.

Chance, Jane. *The Lord of the Rings: The Mythology of Power.* New York: Twayne, 1992.

Crabbe, Katharyn. *J. R. R. Tolkien.* New York: Frederick Ungar, 1981, 1988.

Curry, Patrick. *Defending Middle-earth: Tolkien, Myth, and Modernity.* New York: St. Martin's Press, 1997.

Day, David. *Tolkien: The Illustrated Encyclopedia.* New York: Macmillan, 1991.

———. *Tolkien's Ring.* London: HarperCollins, 1994.

Evans, Robley. *J. R. R. Tolkien.* New York: Warner Books, 1972

Flieger, Verlyn. *A Question of Time: J. R. R. Tolkien's Road to Faërie.* Kent, OH: Kent State University Press, 1997.

———. *Splintered Light: Logos and Language in Tolkien's World.* Grand Rapids, MI: Eerdman's, 1983.

Fonstad, Karen Wynn. *The Atlas of Middle-earth.* Boston: Houghton Mifflin, 1981; rev. 1998.

Foster, Robert. *The Complete Guide to Middle-earth: From* The Hobbit *to* The Silmarillion. New York: Ballantine, 1979.

Giddings, Robert. *J. R. R. Tolkien: The Shores of Middle-earth.* Frederick, MD: Aletheia Books, 1982.

———. *J. R. R. Tolkien: This Far Land.* Totowa, NJ: Barnes and Noble, 1984.

Grotta-Kurska, Daniel. *J. R. R. Tolkien: Architect of Middle Earth.* Philadelphia: Running Press, 1976.

Hammond, Wayne. *J. R. R. Tolkien: A Descriptive Bibliography.* New Castle, DE: Oak Knoll Books, 1993.

Helms, Randel. *Tolkien's World.* Boston: Houghton Mifflin, 1974.

Henning, Jeffrey. "Growing Up with Language," *Model Languages* Vol. 1, No. 8 (Jan.-Feb. 1996).

Isaacs, Neil, and Rose Zimbardo, eds. *Tolkien and the Critics: Essays on J. R. R. Tolkien's* The Lord of the Rings. Notre Dame, IN: University of Notre Dame Press, 1968.

———. eds. *Tolkien: New Critical Perspectives.* Lexington, KY: University Press of Kentucky, 1981.

Johnson, Judith Ann. *J. R. R. Tolkien: Six Decades of Criticism.* Westport, CT: Greenwood Press, 1986.

Kocher, Paul H. *Master of Middle-earth: the Fiction of J. R. R. Tolkien.* Boston: Houghton Mifflin, 1972.

Lobdell, Jared. *England and Always.* Grand Rapids, MI: Eerdmans, 1983.

———, ed. *A Tolkien Compass.* La Salle, IL: Open Court, 1975.

Moseley, Charles. *J. R. R. Tolkien.* Plymouth (UK): Northcote House, 1997.

Nitzsche, Jane Chance. *Tolkien's Art: A Mythology for England.* New York: St. Martin's Press, 1979.

Noel, Ruth S. *The Languages of Tolkien's Middle-earth.* Boston: Houghton Mifflin, 1980.

———. *The Mythology of Middle-earth.* Boston: Houghton Mifflin, 1978.

Pearce, Joseph. *Tolkien: Man and Myth.* London and San Francisco: HarperCollins & Ignatius Press, 1998.

Petty, Anne C. *One Ring to Bind Them All: Tolkien's Mythology.* University, AL: University of Alabama Press, 1979.

Purtill, Richard. *J. R. R. Tolkien: Myth, Morality and Religion.* New York: Harper and Row, 1984.

Rogers, Deborah. *J. R. R. Tolkien.* Boston: Twayne, 1980.

Rosebury, Brian. *Tolkien: A Critical Assessment.* New York: St. Martin's Press, 1992.

Salu, Mary, and Robert T. Farrell, eds. *J. R. R. Tolkien, Scholar and Storyteller: Essays in Memoriam.* Ithaca and London: Cornell University Press, 1979.

Shippey, Tom. *J. R. R. Tolkien: Author of the Century.* Boston: Houghton Mifflin, 2001.

———. *The Road to Middle-earth.* Boston: Houghton Mifflin, 1983.

Strachey, Barbara. *Journeys of Frodo: An Atlas of J. R. R. Tolkien's* The Lord of the Rings. London: HarperCollins, 1981, 1998.

Tolkien, Christopher, ed. *The History of Middle-earth:*
    Volume I: *The Book of Lost Tales, Part I.* Boston: Houghton Mifflin, 1984.
    Volume II: *The Book of Lost Tales, Part II.* Boston: Houghton Mifflin, 1984.
    Volume III: *The Lays of Beleriand.* Boston: Houghton Mifflin, 1985.
    Volume IV: *The Shaping of Middle-earth: The Quenta, The Ambarkanta and the Annals.* Boston: Houghton Mifflin, 1986.
    Volume V: *The Lost Road and Other Writings.* Boston: Houghton Mifflin, 1987.
    Volume VI: *The Return of the Shadow: The History of 'The Lord of the Rings' Part One.* Boston: Houghton Mifflin, 1988.
    Volume VII: *The Treason of Isengard: The History of 'The Lord of the Rings' Part Two.* Boston: Houghton Mifflin, 1989.

Volume VIII: *The War of the Ring: The History of 'The Lord of the Rings' Part Three.* Boston: Houghton Mifflin, 1990.

Volume IX: *Sauron Defeated: The End of the Third Age: The History of 'The Lord of the Rings' Part Four.* Boston: Houghton Mifflin, 1992.

Volume X: *Morgoth's Ring: The Later Silmarillion Part One.*Boston: Houghton Mifflin, 1993.

Volume XI: *The War of the Jewels: The Later Silmarillion Part Two.* Boston: Houghton Mifflin, 1994.

Volume XII: *The Peoples of Middle-earth.* Boston: Houghton Mifflin, 1996.

Tolkien, J. R. R. *The Hobbit.* New York: Ballantine, 1966.

———. *The Lord of the Rings.* New York: Ballantine, 1965.

———. *Poems and Stories.* Boston: Houghton Mifflin, 1994. [Contents nearly identical to those of *The Tolkien Reader;* this collection includes "Smith of Wooton Major"; the other includes an essay, "Tolkien's Magic Ring," by Peter S. Beagle.]

———. *The Silmarillion.* Ed. Christopher Tolkien. Boston: Houghton Mifflin, 1977.

———. *The Tolkien Reader.* New York: Ballantine, 1966.

———. *Unfinished Tales.* Ed. Christopher Tolkien. Boston: Houghton Mifflin, 1980.

The Tolkien Papers. Mankato Studies in English, No. 2. Mankato State University Studies, Vol. II, No. 1. Mankato, MN: February, 1967.

Tyler, J. E. A. *The New Tolkien Companion.* New York: St. Martin's Press, 1979.

West, Richard C. *Tolkien Criticism: An Annotated Checklist.* Rev. ed., Kent, OH: Kent State University Press, 1981.

INDEX